"
Nothing ever tasted
better than a cold beer
on a beautiful afternoon
with nothing to look
forward to than more
of the same.
"

HUGH HOOD
ESSAYIST, PROFESSOR

BEER*MISCUOUS*
2812 North Lincoln Avenue
Chicago, IL 60657

beermiscuous.com

ISBN: 978-0-9989958-0-9

Printed in PRC

BEERMISCUOUS FIELD GUIDE

THE ULTIMATE ADVENTURER'S GUIDE TO
CRAFT BREWERY TAPROOMS + BREWPUBS

BEERMISCUOUS
A Chicago-based craft beer café and retailer.

BEER*MISCUOUS* Adventures
...beyond the café.

Beermiscuous, by definition, is the casual and frequent enjoyment of a wide variety of craft beer. Our unique Chicago "coffee shop for beer" started out in 2014 with the mission to provide a single location for a personal beer exploration in an environment that blended European café elegance with American coffee shop edge.

But along our own journey, we've come to appreciate how valuable the pilgrimage to the source of the beer's creation is to invigorating the spirit of true exploration - both geographic and liquid exploration. Our hope is that this field guide will simplify your journey to Chicago's taprooms and brewpubs*, enhance your experiences, and of course remind you of home (hint: Beermiscuous) once in a while.

*NOTE: this guide is not a comprehensive list to ALL Chicago breweries, but only those where you can drink on the site where the beer is brewed.

CONTRIBUTORS

Mindy Dunn (design)

Andrew Hilsberg (research, editing)

Anna Lindquist (content)

Austin Harvey (content)

Paul Leamon (editing, publishing)

Mike Zoller (content)

TABLE OF CONTENTS

___

HALF ACRE BEER CO.

FIELD NOTES

4257 N. Lincoln Ave.
Chicago, IL 60618
773-248-4038
halfacrebeer.com

Around for nearly a decade, Half Acre qualifies now as one of the old guard of Chicago craft beer. Half Acre started by contract-brewing two beers (a lager and an ESB) in Sand Creek, WI, with the hope of eventually opening a facility in Chicago proper. That day arrived with the acquisition of the Lincoln Avenue facility in 2008. It was several years before they added a taproom and a few years more for a kitchen addition. In 2016, Half Acre opened another production facility on Balmoral in Bowmanville, with the hopes of another taproom to come.

Photo Credit: Brew Bokeh

OWNER
Gabriel Magliaro, Matt Gallagher, Maurizio Fiori, Brian Black

HEAD BREWER
Matt Young

AVAILABILITY
IL, WI, Philadelphia, New York City

BEST KNOWN FOR
Pales, IPAs

DATE FOUNDED
2006

2016 PRODUCTION
36,425 bbl

RECENT AWARDS
FoBAB 2016

KEY EVENTS
Big North (Aug), Big Hugs Release (Dec)

PUBLIC TRANSIT
'L' Brown/Montrose

| 14 | 70 | | | | • | | • | | • | 4.1/5 |

AT-A-GLANCE INFORMATION

# of taps	seating capacity	outdoor seating	pet friendly	kid friendly	TVs	snacks	full menu	off-street parking	transit friendly	rating

HOW TO USE THIS GUIDE IN THE FIELD

HALF ACRE BEER CO.

PRO TIPS
A compilation of beer travelers' advice that will help maximize the enjoyment of your visit.

PRO TIPS

» Small with beautiful wood paneling on the walls and beer hall-style seating.

» Food is a twist on nachos and burritos. Unique, moderately-sized burritos get a culinary twist, while the "Science Cheese" of their now-famous nachos puts the gooey ballpark stuff to shame.

» The facility on Balmoral is production-only, although Half Acre just announced that they've been given approval to build a taproom and restaurant there.

» While kid-friendly, it can get quite crowded and loud during nights and weekends.

» On a weekend be prepared to wait. They are strict with their capacity and will keep people outside in line.

Photo Credit: Brew Bokeh

DATE OF VISIT:

MY RATING
☆ ☆ ☆ ☆ ☆

NOTES:

JOURNAL
A true field guide wouldn't be complete without your own notes on your visit and experiences.

POPULAR BEERS

POPULAR BEERS
Represents a few of the most checked-in beers on social media. May not be available year-round.

M	Tu	W	Th	F	S	Su
closed	11a-11p	11a-11p	11a-12a	11a-1a	11a-1a	11a-11p

HOURS
We advise double checking the hours as these do change frequently.

SUBURBS NORTHWEST

SUBURBS NORTH

SUBURBS FAR WEST

SUBURBS WEST

CITY
(SEE INSET)

SUBURBS SOUTH

NEIGHBORHOODS

CITY
NORTH-
WEST

CITY
NORTH

CITY
NEAR
LOOP

CITY SOUTH

SUBURBS
NORTHWEST
INDIANA

In order to simplify your exploration (and stay true to the identity of Chicago as a community of well defined neighborhoods), we've organized the taprooms and brewpubs by similar geography. Take note that each neighborhood is color coded, which corresponds to the colored stripe along the top of each page.

Additionally, each neighborhood chapter begins with a more detailed map of each area. While the maps do provide some basic road detail, they are not meant to be used for directions. We recommend you use them to help plan out possible stops at two or three taprooms/brewpubs in close proximity to each other. Take advantage of your journey.

Enjoy exploring, be safe, and stay beermiscuous!

CITY NORTH

1. Andersonville Brewing
2. Band of Bohemia
3. Begyle Brewing Co.
4. Burnt City Brewing
5. Corridor Brewery
6. Dovetail Brewery
7. DryHop Brewers
8. Empirical Brewery
9. Greenstar Brewing
10. Half Acre Beer Co.

NEIGHBORHOOD HIGHLIGHTS

Beermiscuous
1 Lincoln Park Zoo
2 Montrose Beach
3 Wrigley Field
4 Old Town School of Folk Music
5 Aragon Ballroom

1

ANDERSONVILLE BREWING

FIELD NOTES

5402 N. Clark St.
Chicago, IL 60640
773-784-6969
**hamburgermarys.
com/chicago/
brewing/**

The purple-and-pink outside of Hamburger Mary's at the corner of Balmoral and Clark is unmistakable, as is the winking lady holding up a massive burger on a plate in the style of your favorite Frisch's or Big Boy diner. This neighborhood burger joint is more than just a place for folks to "Eat, Drink, and be Mary," though. The self-proclaimed "oldest nano-brewery in Chicago," Andersonville Brewing, dates back to 2009 and is the craft brew project of Hamburger Mary's, a longtime mainstay in the Andersonville neighborhood.

OWNER
Brandon Wright,
Ashley Wright

HEAD BREWER
Brandon Wright

AVAILABILITY
Brewpub only

BEST KNOWN FOR
IPAs, sessionable
ales

DATE FOUNDED
2009

2016 PRODUCTION
135 bbl

16 | 76 | • | | | • | • | | • | | 3.3/5

ANDERSONVILLE BREWING

PRO TIPS

» Many beer-themed ingredients featured on the food menu, from the gravy in the poutine to the BBQ sauce.

» A rotating IPA is always available for the hop-heads; barrel-aged beers now and then.

» Advertises as being "one of just a few certified GREEN restaurants in Chicago."

» Kitchen closes a few hours before the bar.

» Weekend brunch available until 3p.

» The Attic, usually open Wednesdays-Sundays, was named one of the best gay bars in the world by OUT Magazine, with live music, cabaret, and dance parties.

DATE OF VISIT:

MY RATING
☆ ☆ ☆ ☆ ☆

NOTES:

POPULAR BEERS

M	Tu	W	Th	F	S	Su
5p-12a	5p-12a	5p-12a	5p-1:30	5p-1:30	12-2:30	12p-12a

BAND OF BOHEMIA

FIELD NOTES

4710 N. Ravenswood Ave.
Chicago, IL 60640
773-271-4710
bandofbohemia.com

The first brewpub to ever win a coveted Michelin star, Band of Bohemia has the most integrated food-and-beer program of any restaurant in the city, perhaps the country. Head brewer and co-founder Michael Carroll began as a chef, working in New England before landing at Chicago's legendary Alinea restaurant in 2006. Half Acre brought him on as a brewer in 2009, and since then his passions and talents have led him to create beers meant to specifically pair with dishes, creating a special dining experience that few restaurants in the world can offer.

OWNER
Craig Sindelar,
Michael Carroll

HEAD BREWER
Michael Carroll

AVAILABILITY
Chicago - limited

BEST KNOWN FOR
Food inspired ales
with spices and
fruits

DATE FOUNDED
2015

2016 PRODUCTION
400 bbl

RECENT AWARDS
Michelin starred

KEY EVENTS
Caravan Art Festival
(Sept)

PUBLIC TRANSIT
'L' Brown/Damen,
UP-N/Ravenswood

8	150			•			•	•		3.8/5

BAND OF BOHEMIA

PRO TIPS

» Features a pre-fixe, multi-course meal with beers spotlighting adjunct spices designed to pair with each course.
» Not your typical brewery/brewpub.
» Atmosphere is almost akin to a fancy Viennese salon, featuring artwork by Chicago artist Elizabeth Weber
» Upscale but approachable and unpretentious.
» While reservations aren't required, we recommend making one.
» There are specific times the kitchen is closed but the bar is open, so double check hours ahead of time if you're hoping to eat.

DATE OF VISIT:

MY RATING
☆ ☆ ☆ ☆ ☆

NOTES:

POPULAR BEERS

| Orange Chicory Rye | The Culinary Noble |

M	Tu	W	Th	F	S	Su
closed	4:30-12	4:30-12	4:30-12	4:30-12	11a-1a	11a-10p

⋁ BEGYLE BREWING CO.

FIELD NOTES

1800 W. Cuyler Ave.
Chicago, IL 60613
773-661-6963
begylebrewing.com

Around since 2011, Begyle's space along Ravenswood Avenue in Chicago's North Center neighborhood is one of many breweries that occupy former industrial buildings next to the railroad tracks. This particular popular area is now called Malt Row. The brewery's name stems from the fact that they originally wanted to open on Argyle Avenue, about a mile north of their current location. When that plan fell through, one could say they went with plan B. Begyle's flagship beers are very approachable, with some higher-octane options usually available.

OWNER
Kevin Cary

HEAD BREWER
Liz French

AVAILABILITY
Chicago

BEST KNOWN FOR
Blondes, hoppy ales, stouts

DATE FOUNDED
2011

2016 PRODUCTION
1,811 bbl

KEY EVENTS
Imperial Pajamas Release (Nov)

PUBLIC TRANSIT
'L' Brown/Irving Park

| 13 | 60 | | | • | | • | | | | | | • | | 4.0/5 |

BEGYLE BREWING CO.

PRO TIPS

- » Taproom is small but welcoming, with almost a coffee shop vibe to it when it's not too crowded.
- » Expect to find plenty of neighborhood residents here, but no seating at the bar.
- » Tours are a good deal. $10 gets you an hour and a half-long tour, a glass, and three beers. Tours are on Saturdays at noon.
- » A CSB (community-supported brewery) program is available that gets members regular growler pours for 6- or 12-month periods for an upfront fee.
- » There's a skeeball table in the taproom that sees plenty of use.
- » Food trucks most weekends.

DATE OF VISIT:

MY RATING
☆ ☆ ☆ ☆ ☆

NOTES:

POPULAR BEERS

M	Tu	W	Th	F	S	Su
12p-9p	12p-9p	12p-9p	12p-9p	12p-10p	11a-12a	12p-8p

BURNT CITY BREWING

FIELD NOTES

2747 N. Lincoln Ave.
Chicago, IL 60614
773-295-1270
burntcitybrewing.com

Referencing the Great Chicago Fire of 1871, Burnt City Brewing is the continuation of what was Atlas Brewing. Founded in 2012, Atlas was forced to change names in 2015, and the phoenix that rose from those ashes was Burnt City. Head pub brewer Christian Burd supplements a list of several perennial beers brewed in their south side Chicago production brewery with some uniquely marvelous creations at the pub. Knowing the neighborhood of younger professionals and exuberant craft beer novices, Burd isn't afraid of fruit beers, either.

OWNER
John Saller, Ben Saller

HEAD BREWER
Christian Burd

AVAILABILITY
AL, IL, IN, MI, MO

BEST KNOWN FOR
IPAs, pales, wheat ales

DATE FOUNDED
2012

2016 PRODUCTION
1,150 bbl

KEY EVENTS
Craft Beer Prom (May), New Year's Eve Party (Dec)

PUBLIC TRANSIT
'L' Brown/Diversey

25 | 200 | • | | • | • | | • | | • | 3.6/5

BURNT CITY BREWING

PRO TIPS

» The adjacent Seven Ten lounge is a stylish, hip bowling alley that allows you a way to burn off the beer you consume, and impress your friends.

» Features upscale takes on classic pub fare, including totchos (think nachos, but with tater tots replacing the tortilla chips), chicharrones (Mexican-style pork cracklins), pizzas (try the white pizza with stout-braised mushrooms) and BBQ (the burnt ends go great with a barrel-aged brew).

» Production brewery is on the south side of Chicago and does not offer tours or a tap room.

» The closest brewery to your favorite journey launchpad - Beermiscuous.

DATE OF VISIT:

MY RATING

☆ ☆ ☆ ☆ ☆

NOTES:

POPULAR BEERS

M	Tu	W	Th	F	S	Su
5p-11p	5p-11p	5p-11p	5p-11p	5p-2a	12p-2a	12p-11p

CORRIDOR BREWERY & PROVISIONS

FIELD NOTES

3446 N. Southport Ave.
Chicago, IL 60657
773-270-4272
corridorchicago.com

The sister pub to East Lakeview's DryHop Brewers, Corridor Brewery & Provisions resides on the western side of Lakeview in a mini-neighborhood known as the Southport Corridor. Perhaps a little more upscale than DryHop (but absolutely befitting of the neighborhood), Corridor is the place to go if you want a classy atmosphere to enjoy a nice meal for a date or with the family while drinking a beer named Zombie Eater Saison. The house beer selections are brewed to season, so don't expect to see an imperial stout in the middle of summer.

OWNER
Greg Shuff

HEAD BREWER
Brant Dubovick

AVAILABILITY
Brewpub only

BEST KNOWN FOR
IPAs, saisons, sours

DATE FOUNDED
2015

2016 PRODUCTION
800 bbl

KEY EVENTS
Anniversary Party (Oct)

PUBLIC TRANSIT
'L' Brown/Southport

6 | 90 | • | • | • | | | | • | | • | 3.8/5

CORRIDOR BREWERY & PROVISIONS

PRO TIPS

» Dog friendly on the patio only.

» No reservations are taken here, so show up early or plan for a wait if you're coming during an evening, a weekend or brunch.

» Menu features multiple mussels preparations, clay-oven pizzas, shared plates, salads, and sandwiches, all lovingly considered.

» On Mondays you can get their burger (which is really good), a pint and a shot for $15. Every Saturday they have $7 growler fills for one specific beer.

» Weekly Tuesday Beer & Vinyl events.

» Nearby visits should be made to the Mercury Theater, Music Box, and numerous boutiques and shops along Southport Ave.

DATE OF VISIT:

MY RATING
☆ ☆ ☆ ☆ ☆

NOTES:

POPULAR BEERS

Wizard Fight	Freaky Deaky	Nibble Nibble Little Mouse	First Daze Here

M	Tu	W	Th	F	S	Su
11a-11p	11a-11p	11a-12a	11a-12a	11a-12a	10a-12a	10a-11p

DOVETAIL BREWERY

FIELD NOTES

Dovetail is one of the buzzier new breweries in the city. It's the brainchild of Hagen Dost and Bill Wesselink, who came up with the idea as they studied brewing at the Doemens Akademie in Munich. Located, like many Chicago breweries, in an old industrial building, the idea of craftsmanship that colored older methods of manufacture is still held to an ideal here. The brewery features a copper vessel re-purposed from the pilot system at Weihenstephaner, the world's oldest continuously-functioning brewery, in Bavaria.

1800 W. Belle Plaine Ave.
Chicago, IL 60613
773-683-1414
dovetailbrewery.com

OWNER
Hagen Dost, Bill Wesselink

HEAD BREWER
Hagen Dost, Bill Wesselink

AVAILABILITY
Chicago - draft only

BEST KNOWN FOR
German style lagers, wheat ales

DATE FOUNDED
2015

2016 PRODUCTION
445 bbl

KEY EVENTS
Maifest (May), Oktoberfest (Sept)

PUBLIC TRANSIT
'L' Brown/Irving Park

18 | 90 | • | • | • | • | MENU | • | • | 4.1/5

DOVETAIL BREWERY

PRO TIPS

» Outdoor picnic tables are only available on Saturday and Sunday.

» Take the brewery tour here (usually on Saturday afternoons). The copper vessel shipped over from Germany, and the story behind it, are both fascinating and worth every moment of time spent talking about it.

» House-blended radlers are available that marry house beers with light sodas. If you're feeling adventurous, try the Rauchbier (smoked beer), or better yet, try a radler made with it; you've never had anything like it before.

» Food trucks come by occasionally.

» Space can fill up fast, but wait for a tour to start, then grab a table.

DATE OF VISIT:

MY RATING
☆ ☆ ☆ ☆ ☆

NOTES:

POPULAR BEERS

| Lager | Hefewei-zen | Rauch-bier | Dunkel-weizen |

M	Tu	W	Th	F	S	Su
closed	2p-10p	2p-10p	2p-10p	12p-11p	11a-11p	12p-8p

DRYHOP BREWERS

FIELD NOTES

DryHop is located not far from the Boystown area of Lakeview, one of the first municipally-recognized gay neighborhoods anywhere in the country. There's plenty of foot traffic in this area that has a bevy of restaurants, bars, boutiques and independently-owned businesses. DryHop is only a mile away from Wrigley Field and it has quickly become a neighborhood landmark thanks to its well-regarded food menu and frequent beer releases and collaborations.

3155 N. Broadway
Chicago, IL 60657
773-857-3155
dryhopchicago.com

OWNER
Greg Shuff

HEAD BREWER
Brant Dubovick

AVAILABILITY
Brewpub only

BEST KNOWN FOR
Wheat ales, IPAs, stouts

DATE FOUNDED
2013

2016 PRODUCTION
1,100 bbl

KEY EVENTS
Anniversary Party (Jun)

PUBLIC TRANSIT
'L' Red, Brown or Purple/Belmont

6	75	•	•	•			•		•	3.8/5

DRYHOP BREWERS

PRO TIPS

» Dog friendly on the patio only.
» When the windows and patio are open here, DryHop seems like the coolest place in town.
» Weekly Monday Barman's Banquet special ($15 for burger, pint, and shot of bourbon).
» DryHop's sister pub, Corridor Brewery & Provisions, is just a mile west.
» Not a lot of seating and the bar area is very small. Expect to wait a bit when the sun is shining and people are out and about.
» Head Brewer Brant Dubovick is a decorated brewmaster with over a decade of experience and a GABF gold medal on his résumé.

DATE OF VISIT:

MY RATING
☆ ☆ ☆ ☆ ☆

NOTES:

POPULAR BEERS

Shark Meets Hipster	Milksta-chio	The Angry Samoan	Too Many Puppies

M	Tu	W	Th	F	S	Su
11a-12a	11a-12a	11a-12a	11a-12a	11a-2a	11a-2a	11a-12a

EMPIRICAL BREWERY

FIELD NOTES

Science-themed brews with a nod toward experimentation is the name of the game for Empirical with delightfully drinkable results. Each Thursday they release a new beer in the taproom direct from their pilot brewing system. This original location in Ravenswood (a Rogers Park brewpub is coming soon) features a cinder block, big TV, and Christmas light vibe that resembles one's personification of an idealized dorm room. These words make it sound dumpy, but to be assured, it is not. Empirical keeps it very clean and the space is incredibly charming.

1801 W. Foster Ave.
Chicago, IL 60640
773-654-3104
empiricalbrewery.com

OWNER
Bill Hurley

HEAD BREWER
Jacob Huston

AVAILABILITY
Chicago

BEST KNOWN FOR
IPAs, robust dark ales

DATE FOUNDED
2014

2016 PRODUCTION
1,000 bbl

KEY EVENTS
Black Wednesday Party (Nov), Anniversary Party (Nov)

PUBLIC TRANSIT
'L' Red/Morse

12 | 95 | · | · | · | · | · | 3.9/5

EMPIRICAL BREWERY

PRO TIPS

» The brewery houses a small cat colony. So, if you have a cat allergy, you might want to take an antihistamine before visiting.

» The taproom is dog friendly (the cats are separated away in the brewhouse).

» Brewery tours are every Saturday at 12:30, no reservations, and they advertise a chance to potentially meet the cats.

» A second location (brewpub with food) is on Morse Avenue in Rogers Park and scheduled to open in Summer 2017.

» Every Friday they tap a unique firkin.

» Features live music occasionally.

DATE OF VISIT:

MY RATING
☆ ☆ ☆ ☆ ☆

NOTES:

POPULAR BEERS

M	Tu	W	Th	F	S	Su
closed	12p-10p	12p-10p	12p-12a	12p-12a	12p-12a	12p-8p

GREENSTAR BREWING

FIELD NOTES

3800 N. Clark St.
Chicago, IL 60013
773-929-3680
**uncommonground.
com/green-
star-brewing**

Uncommon Ground/Greenstar Brewing, in the Wrigleyville neighborhood, is a bit of an anomaly in an area that can get absolutely bonkers on game days. This classy restaurant and bar a couple of blocks north of Wrigley Field is a destination for the neighborhood's population of young professionals and Cubs fans looking for a more laid-back game day experience. As a natural extension to their local, organic and sustainable ideals, Uncommon Ground launched the 7-barrel brewery Greenstar in 2014, as the first certified organic brewery in Illinois.

OWNER
Michael Cameron,
Helen Cameron

HEAD BREWER
Martin Coad

AVAILABILITY
Brewpub only

BEST KNOWN FOR
IPAs, pales, stouts,
Kölsch

DATE FOUNDED
2014

2016 PRODUCTION
N/A

KEY EVENTS
Oktoberfest
(Sept), 12 Beers of
Christmas (Dec)

PUBLIC TRANSIT
'L' Red/Addison

| 12 | 150 | • | | • | | • | | | | • | | | • | 3.5/5 |

GREENSTAR BREWING

PRO TIPS

» Dog friendly on the patio only.

» What Greenstar's beers might lack in bonkers experimentalism they more than make up for in environmental and food-friendliness.

» Operates two independently-owned restaurants in the city. A second location is on the northern side of the Edgewater neighborhood on Devon Avenue, not far from Loyola University. These are the only two locations where you'll find Greenstar.

» The food menu has plenty of vegetarian and vegan options, as well as some gluten-free dishes.

» Very popular weekend brunch.

» Located steps away from two premier music venues: Metro and Smart Bar.

POPULAR BEERS

Space-ship IPA	Mutti's	Monk's Libation	Certifi-able Pale Ale

DATE OF VISIT:

MY RATING
☆ ☆ ☆ ☆ ☆

NOTES:

M	Tu	W	Th	F	S	Su
11a-9p	11a-9p	11a-9p	11a-9p	11a-11p	9a-11p	9a-11p

HALF ACRE BEER CO.

FIELD NOTES

4257 N. Lincoln Ave.
Chicago, IL 60618
773-248-4038
halfacrebeer.com

Around for nearly a decade, Half Acre qualifies now as one of the old guard of Chicago craft beer. Half Acre started by contract-brewing two beers (a lager and an ESB) in Sand Creek, WI, with the hope of eventually opening a facility in Chicago proper. That day arrived with the acquisition of the Lincoln Avenue facility in 2008. It was several years before they added a taproom and a few years more for a kitchen addition. In 2016, Half Acre opened another production facility on Balmoral in Bowmanville, with the hopes of another taproom to come.

Photo Credit: Brew Bokeh

OWNER
Gabriel Magliaro, Matt Gallagher, Maurizio Fiori, Brian Black

HEAD BREWER
Matt Young

AVAILABILITY
IL, WI, Philadelphia, New York City

BEST KNOWN FOR
Pales, IPAs

DATE FOUNDED
2006

2016 PRODUCTION
36,425 bbl

RECENT AWARDS
FoBAB 2016

KEY EVENTS
Big North (Aug), Big Hugs Release (Dec)

PUBLIC TRANSIT
'L' Brown/Montrose

| 14 | 70 | | | | • | | | | • | | • | 4.1/5 |

HALF ACRE BEER CO.

PRO TIPS

» Small with beautiful wood paneling on the walls and beer hall-style seating.

» Food is a twist on nachos and burritos. Unique, moderately-sized burritos get a culinary twist, while the "Science Cheese" of their now-famous nachos puts the gooey ballpark stuff to shame.

» The facility on Balmoral is production-only, although Half Acre just announced that they've been given approval to build a taproom and restaurant there.

» While kid-friendly, it can get quite crowded and loud during nights and weekends.

» On a weekend be prepared to wait. They are strict with their capacity and will keep people outside in line.

POPULAR BEERS

Photo Credit: Brew Bokeh

DATE OF VISIT:

MY RATING
☆ ☆ ☆ ☆ ☆

NOTES:

M	Tu	W	Th	F	S	Su
closed	11a-11p	11a-11p	11a-12a	11a-1a	11a-1a	11a-11p

CITY NORTHWEST

1. Alarmist Brewing
2. Hopewell Brewing Co.
3. Old Irving Brewing Co.
4. Piece Brewery & Pizzeria
5. Revolution Brewing

NEIGHBORHOOD HIGHLIGHTS

1 The 606 Trail
2 Bang Bang Pie Shop
3 Basilica of St. Hyacinth
4 Irish American Heritage Center

North

ALARMIST BREWING

FIELD NOTES

Gary Gulley started with homebrewing over 25 years ago, but his passion only fully took hold of him in 2015. Opting more for quality over quantity, Alarmist has been perfecting recipes on their core lines of beers as opposed to producing as many beers in as many possible styles as they can. Now, they finally have a taproom to call their own, in the well-to-do, formerly-dry Sauganash neighborhood. The space occupies the former site of the Siebel Institute of Technology, North America's premier brewing school.

4055 W. Peterson Ave.
Chicago, IL 60646
773-681-0877
alarmistbrewing.com

OWNER
Gary Gulley

HEAD BREWER
Aaron Dahl

AVAILABILITY
Chicago

BEST KNOWN FOR
IPAs, pales, Belgian singles

DATE FOUNDED
2015

2016 PRODUCTION
750 bbl

12	70		•	•		•		•		3.8/5

ALARMIST BREWING

PRO TIPS

» The Sauganash ~~neighb~~orhood has an almost-suburban feel to it.

» For cyclists, the brewery is right off the Sauganash Trail, a re-purposed 1-mile railway bridge that goes between Devon and Bryn Mawr Avenues. The North Branch (on the west of Alarmist) and North Shore Channel (on the east) bike trails are both within reasonable distances from Alarmist.

» Taproom does not currently accept cash, so make sure you have a credit card on you.

» Formerly known as Panic Brewing.

» Ask the owner, Gary, if he's there, how much of the taproom he built with his own hands.

DATE OF VISIT:

MY RATING
☆ ☆ ☆ ☆ ☆

NOTES:

POPULAR BEERS

M	Tu	W	Th	F	S	Su
4p-11p	4p-11p	4p-11p	4p-11p	12p-12a	11a-12a	12p-10p

HOPEWELL BREWING CO.

FIELD NOTES

2760 N. Milwaukee Ave.
Chicago, IL 60647
773-698-6178
hopewellbrewing.com

The influx of new, young people into Logan Square has meant a lot of thirsty folks clamoring for beer. On the northwest edge of the neighborhood, this fairly new taproom is a nexus for the area's discerning beverage crowd. The main focus of Hopewell Brewing is on balanced, utilitarian beers; so don't expect face-puckering, enamel-peeling sours or tongue-lashing, hyper-bitter IPAs. Instead, expect to drink beers here that you wouldn't mind having several of during an afternoon.

OWNER
Jonathan Fritz,
Samantha Lee,
Stephen Bossu

HEAD BREWER
Stephen Bossu

AVAILABILITY
Chicago

BEST KNOWN FOR
Balanced beers,
lagers, IPAs, kettle
sours

DATE FOUNDED
2016

2016 PRODUCTION
N/A

RECENT AWARDS
FoBAB 2016

KEY EVENTS
Anniversary Party
(Feb)

PUBLIC TRANSIT
'L' Blue/Logan
Square

| 10 | 99 | | | • | | • | | | | | | • | 3.8/5 |

HOPEWELL BREWING CO.

PRO TIPS

» Space is decent-sized but can fill up quickly. Crowds will get big on some nights, but the atmosphere is generally accommodating and friendly.

» A few reservations are taken on a day-to-day basis.

» Food trucks and restaurant pop-ups will happen occasionally, but make sure to check in advance.

» A nice selection of board games are available while you drink.

» It's a very well lit, bright modern space. Big windows let you look into the brewhouse.

» Perfect spot for a drink before or after a movie at the nearby Logan Theatre.

DATE OF VISIT:

MY RATING

NOTES:

POPULAR BEERS

| Farm and Family Saison | Cold Brew |

M	Tu	W	Th	F	S	Su
closed	4p-11p	4p-11p	4p-11p	4p-12a	12p-12a	12p-11p

OLD IRVING BREWING CO.

FIELD NOTES

4419 W. Montrose Ave.
Chicago, IL 60641
773-916-6421
oldirvingbrewing.com

In a residential neighborhood that is starting to see its fair share of families move in, it's no surprise that a top-notch brewpub would open up in Old Irving Park. It's not often that a brewpub's food is on par with its beer, at least when the beer is this excellent. And yet, Old Irving Brewery's menu is among the best of all brewpubs in the city, with its adventurous-yet-approachable dining options rivaling Trevor Rose-Hamblin's remarkable beers. Many popular Chicago publications seem to wholeheartedly agree.

OWNER
Trevor Rose-
Hamblin, Jeff
Linnemeyer,
Matthias Merges

HEAD BREWER
Trevor Rose-Hamblin

AVAILABILITY
Brewpub only

BEST KNOWN FOR
IPAs, stouts,
Belgians, lighter ales

DATE FOUNDED
2016

2016 PRODUCTION
N/A

PUBLIC TRANSIT
'L' Blue/Montrose

| 20 | 225 | | | | • | | • | | | • | | | • | 3.9/5 |

OLD IRVING BREWING CO.

PRO TIPS

» Special bottle releases will happen at the pub every now and then; call in advance to see when the next one is.

» The sandwiches and entrées are all fabulous, but the small plates, like the fried zucchini strips and shishito peppers, are not to be missed.

» Every Monday they have a new featured burger, beer, and bourbon for $15.

» Does not take reservations, so for more popular hours, expect a wait.

» Great place to bring the family. Brewery visible from the dining area.

» 14 TVs and a 10' big screen for just about any sporting event.

» Yoga on select weekend mornings in the brewery.

DATE OF VISIT:

MY RATING
☆ ☆ ☆ ☆ ☆

NOTES:

POPULAR BEERS

| Scentinel | Black Monday | Guten Tag | Krampus Cookies |

M	Tu	W	Th	F	S	Su
5p-11p	5p-11p	5p-11p	5p-11p	3p-1a	11a-1a	11a-10p

PIECE BREWERY & PIZZERIA

FIELD NOTES

1927 W. North Ave.
Chicago, IL 60622
773-772-4422
piecechicago.com

Rick Nielsen (guitarist in Rock and Roll Hall of Fame inductee Cheap Trick) is a part owner of this Wicker Park mainstay. Sometimes Nielsen's famous five-necked guitar will be on display in this restaurant with beautiful exposed bow truss architectural features. Brewmaster Jonathan Cutler (no relation to the former Bears' quarterback, which is probably a good thing in this town) has won several deserved awards for his quaffable, flavorful beers that always seem to go well with the New Haven-style pizzas.

OWNER
Bill Jacobs

HEAD BREWER
Jonathan Cutler

AVAILABILITY
Brewpub only

BEST KNOWN FOR
Pale ales, German wheat ales, lighter ales

DATE FOUNDED
2001

2016 PRODUCTION
1,750 bbl

RECENT AWARDS
GABF 2016

KEY EVENTS
Festivus (Nov)

PUBLIC TRANSIT
'L' Blue/Damen

16 | 275 | | | • | • | | • | | • | 3.9/5

PIECE BREWERY & PIZZERIA

PRO TIPS

» The pizza here is New Haven-style, which means thin crusts, oblong-shaped pies, and super-hot oven temperatures leading to charred crusts.

» They have brunch pizzas on Saturday and Sunday.

» Don't miss the special pizza of the month with a local "celebrity" like Doug Sohn of now-closed Hot Doug's.

» Fun fact: the Cheetah Gym across the street used to be the home of MTV's The Real World.

» Will get busy during weekend evenings and big sporting events, so don't plan to find a seat immediately.

» Live band karaoke on Saturdays at 11p.

DATE OF VISIT:

MY RATING
☆ ☆ ☆ ☆ ☆

NOTES:

POPULAR BEERS

| The Weight | Camel Toe | Camel Toe | Top Heavy Hefeweizen |

M	Tu	W	Th	F	S	Su
11a-12a	11a-12a	11a-12a	11a-12a	11a-2a	11a-2a	11a-11p

REVOLUTION BREWING

FIELD NOTES

3340 N. Kedzie Ave.
Chicago, IL 60618
773-588-2267
revbrew.com

Illinois's largest independently-owned brewery, Revolution is the brainchild of Josh Deth, who opened the eclectic, vegetarian-friendly restaurant Handlebar in Wicker Park in 2003. After a few failed attempts, Deth opened a Logan Square brewpub off the California Blue Line stop in 2010 - the original Revolution Brewing location. The success of that space, and its subsequent expansion to the second floor of its building, led to the construction and opening of the Kedzie production facility and taproom in 2012. By 2016, Revolution was among the 50 largest craft brewers in the country.

OWNER
Josh Deth

HEAD BREWER
Jim Cibak, Wil Turner

AVAILABILITY
IL, IN, MA, OH, WI, New York City

BEST KNOWN FOR
IPAs, lighter styles

DATE FOUNDED
2010

2016 PRODUCTION
71,580 bbl

RECENT AWARDS
FoBAB 2016, WBC 2016

PUBLIC TRANSIT
'L' Blue/Belmont

16 | 281 | | • | • | • | • | 4.5/5

REVOLUTION BREWING

PRO TIPS

» Taproom closes for private events somewhat regularly, so be sure to check Revolution's social media or call ahead to make sure they'll be open.

» While Kedzie (described here) is the main production house, Revolution's brewpub is a little over a mile south (2323 N. Milwaukee Ave.) where you can occassionally find a different selection of Revolution beer.

» Very large industrial space with barrels located right in the taproom, which gives it cool asthetics.

» Free street parking is easy.

» The 2013 movie "Drinking Buddies" starring Olivia Wilde, Jake Johnson and Anna Kendrick was primarily filmed at the taproom.

DATE OF VISIT:

MY RATING

NOTES:

POPULAR BEERS

M	Tu	W	Th	F	S	Su
closed	closed	2p-10p	2p-10p	2p-11p	12p-11p	12p-6p

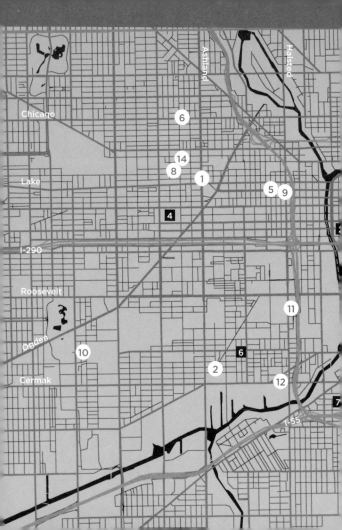

CITY NEAR LOOP

1. All Rise Brewing Co.
2. Alulu
3. Baderbräu
4. Birreria at Eataly Chicago
5. Cruz Blanca Cerveceria
6. Forbidden Root
7. Gino's Brewing Co.
8. Goose Island Beer Co.
9. Haymarket Pub & Brewery
10. Lagunitas Brewing Company
11. Mad Mouse Brewing
12. Moody Tongue Brewing Company
13. Motor Row Brewing
14. On Tour Brewing Co.
15. Vice District Brewing Co.

NEIGHBORHOOD HIGHLIGHTS

1 Navy Pier
2 Willis Tower
3 Michigan Ave. Shopping
4 United Center
5 Museum Campus
6 Thalia Hall
7 Chinatown

ALL RISE BREWING CO.

FIELD NOTES

After years of running one of Chicago's largest music festivals (Riot Fest) and one of its more notorious punk bars (Cobra Lounge), Sean McKeough started a brewery. All Rise might be the first brewery in the country built alongside a punk bar. Head Brewer Tommy Nicely brews styles that are all very approachable and drinkable. Overall, All Rise is the logical extension of a hospitality project of some punks who want to make some beer they want to drink themselves.

235 N. Ashland Ave.
Chicago, IL 60607
312-226-6300
allrisebrewing.com

OWNER
All Rise Brewing

HEAD BREWER
Tommy Nicely

AVAILABILITY
Chicago - very limited draft only

BEST KNOWN FOR
IPAs, wheat ales

DATE FOUNDED
2014

2016 PRODUCTION
1,150 bbl

RECENT AWARDS
WBC 2016

KEY EVENTS
Motoblot (Jun)

PUBLIC TRANSIT
'L' Green or Pink/ Ashland

20 | 300 | • | • | • | | • | • | • | 3.8/5

ALL RISE BREWING CO.

PRO TIPS

» One of the nicest and largest outdoor patios of any brewery within the city limits. Dog friendly on patio only.

» The Lounge hosts concerts on a regular basis, so this is your place to catch some tunes while sampling some brews (plan on the music being LOUD).

» Close enough to On Tour and Goose Island that visiting all three is conceivable in an afternoon, even without a vehicle.

» Food specials Monday through Thursday. Menu is hearty pub grub with a focus on local sourcing.

» You certainly don't need to be a punk in order to enjoy All Rise, but it won't hurt if you can name a Naked Raygun album or two.

POPULAR BEERS

DATE OF VISIT:

MY RATING
☆ ☆ ☆ ☆ ☆

NOTES:

M	Tu	W	Th	F	S	Su
11a-2a	11a-2a	11a-2a	11a-2a	11a-2a	5p-3a	closed

ALULU

FIELD NOTES

BREWPUB
CHI, ILL

2011 S. Laflin St.
Chicago, IL 60608
312-600-9865
alulubrew.com

Alulu is the maiden project of Jeff Hedin (chef), Frank Costanzo and Nancy Rockwood (brewers). Each has drawn on their expertise and enthusiasm to create a wholly unique and idiosyncratic melange of food and beer on the near south side of the city. Despite just opening, Alulu boasts an impressive 11 beers on its draft lines already, all with names meant to evoke science fiction and fantasy genres. Rockwood's worldly travels have led to a love of Belgian and malt-driven ales that can exist without excessive hops.

OWNER
A collective of indie artists & brewers

HEAD BREWER
Logan Helton, Frank Costanzo, Nancy Rockwood, Ryan Metz

AVAILABILITY
Brewpub only

BEST KNOWN FOR
IPAs, Belgians

DATE FOUNDED
2017

2016 PRODUCTION
N/A

PUBLIC TRANSIT
'L' Pink/18th Street

30 | 75 | • | | • | | | • | | • | NA/5

ALULU

PRO TIPS

» In the future, look for barrel-aged and wild-fermented beers to make an appearance.

» Alulu boasts a fireplace for colder weather, and large garage-style door to be opened during warmer weather.

» The restaurant's house beverage program include a line of in-house made sodas that can be consumed separately, or combined as a shandy into one of the house brews. Cocktails and beertails are also available.

» The food menu is eclectic and dynamic, with Jeff Hedin's creations ranging from house-made sausages and pierogi to mussels with frites and vegan egg rolls.

DATE OF VISIT:

MY RATING
☆ ☆ ☆ ☆ ☆

NOTES:

POPULAR BEERS

| Jaunt Rotation | Halcyon Equinox | Libra Aura | Rue Envoy |

M	Tu	W	Th	F	S	Su
closed	closed	closed	5p-12a	5p-12a	5p-12a	5p-12a

BADERBRÄU

FIELD NOTES

2515 S. Wabash Ave.
Chicago, IL 60616
312-890-2728
baderbrau.com

Baderbräu's journey is a winding one. Starting around the same time as Goose Island in the late 1980s, Baderbräu's Chicago Pilsner was a local favorite in the burgeoning craft beer boom of the 1990s. Over-ambition and over-expansion led to hard times for Baderbräu, whose parent company declared bankruptcy in 1997. Goose Island took up the Baderbräu mantle, brewing the famous Chicago Pilsner for a short time before Rob Sama acquired the name, recipe, and yeast strain in 2010. He's been expanding the German-inspired, lager-centric beers ever since.

OWNER
Rob Sama

HEAD BREWER
Nathan Tertell

AVAILABILITY
Chicago

BEST KNOWN FOR
Lagers, American takes on German styles

DATE FOUNDED
2012

2016 PRODUCTION
7,750 bbl

KEY EVENTS
South Side Beer Fest (May)

PUBLIC TRANSIT
'L' Red or Green/ Cermak-McCormick Place

| 10 | 162 | | | • | • | | • | | • | 3.9/5 |

BADERBRÄU

PRO TIPS

» The newly-opened kitchen at the taproom features sandwiches and shareable appetizers, including something called a "Mac & Cheese Waffle" that begs to be experienced in person.

» Baderbrau's upstairs taproom is spacious, with plenty of room at the bar and a number of tables to accommodate a larger group if necessary.

» They are very proud of their South Side location. They brew a beer called South Side Pride and are big fans of the Chicago White Sox.

» Their space is very popular for weddings and other private events, so call ahead to ensure they're open.

DATE OF VISIT:

MY RATING
☆ ☆ ☆ ☆ ☆

NOTES:

POPULAR BEERS

M	Tu	W	Th	F	S	Su
3p-11p	3p-11p	3p-11p	12p-12a	12p-12a	12p-12a	3p-11p

BIRRERIA AT EATALY CHICAGO

FIELD NOTES

BIRRERIA

43 E. Ohio St.
Chicago, IL 60611
312-521-8700
**eataly.com/chica-
go-birreria/**

Mario Batali's Eataly project has led to massive shopping complexes domestically and internationally. The popular destinations traffic in all things Italian food, including fresh pastas, groceries, wines, coffee, and desserts. What sometimes doesn't get mentioned in the conversation about Italy's wonderful food culture is the growing fascination and integration of beer. At Birreria, one will find a couple unique house brews and a well-curated selection of guest drafts.

OWNER
Mario Batali,
Joe Bastianich,
Lidia Matticchio
Bastianich

HEAD BREWER
Eric Dixon

AVAILABILITY
Brewpub only

BEST KNOWN FOR
Belgians, IPAs

DATE FOUNDED
2013

2016 PRODUCTION
300 bbl

PUBLIC TRANSIT
'L' Red/Grand

| 9 | 50 | | | • | | • | | 3.7/5 |

BIRRERIA AT EATALY CHICAGO

PRO TIPS

» No reservations for the Birreria restaurant, first-come first-served only.

» Birreria usually features more guest brews than house brews, but the curation (including a large bottle list) is carefully considered and well-thought out.

» Sam Calagione of Dogfish Head and Teo Musso of Italy's Birra Baladin are partners in the Birreria beer program.

» Steps from the Magnificent Mile of Michigan Avenue, with tons of shopping and entertainment options nearby.

» All televised Chicago Fire soccer games are shown on the TV's.

DATE OF VISIT:

MY RATING
☆ ☆ ☆ ☆ ☆

NOTES:

POPULAR BEERS

| Aria | Manda-rina | Birra-misu |

M	Tu	W	Th	F	S	Su
closed	closed	closed	closed	11a-10p	11a-10p	11a-9p

CRUZ BLANCA CERVECERIA

FIELD NOTES

904 W. Randolph St.
Chicago, IL 60607
312-733-1975
cruzblanca.com

Rick Bayless, one of the true titans of Chicago's restaurant scene, took special care and made no shortcuts when opening his first brewpub. Cruz Blanca is located in the hip West Loop neighborhood, on the stretch of Randolph Street near plenty of other notable restaurants, cocktail bars, and nightlife. Like many other Rick Bayless restaurants, the cuisine is Mexican street-food inspired, with fresh-made tacos and other Oaxacan specialties. The beers themselves are inspired by Mexican-style craft lagers and Mexican food ingredients.

OWNER
Manny Valdes, Rick Bayless

HEAD BREWER
Jacob Sembrano

AVAILABILITY
Brewpub only

BEST KNOWN FOR
Mexican style lagers, food infused beers

DATE FOUNDED
2016

KEY EVENTS
Anniversary Party (May), Cinco de Mayo (May), Das Bueno Oktoberfest (Sept), New Year's Eve (Dec)

PUBLIC TRANSIT
'L' Green or Pink/ Morgan

| 12 | 67 | • | • | • | | | • | • | 3.8/5 |

CRUZ BLANCA CERVECERIA

PRO TIPS

» Dog friendly on the patio only.

» Rated #4 new brewery in the U.S. by USA Today in 2016.

» Limited to-go bottles can sometimes be purchased on-site.

» Like many other West Loop destinations with good beer, Cruz Blanca will fill up with the post-work crowd on many weeknights after 5p, so go during afternoons or on weekends when there's no work crowd.

» If you take a seat at the bar, you can order food there; no need to stand in the food line.

» Large upstairs room with another bar is open Thursday to Saturday nights.

DATE OF VISIT:

MY RATING
☆ ☆ ☆ ☆ ☆

NOTES:

POPULAR BEERS

| Básica | La Guardia Rubia | Winnow | El Train IPA |

M	Tu	W	Th	F	S	Su
closed	11a-10p	11a-10p	11a-10p	11a-12a	11a-12a	11a-9p

FORBIDDEN ROOT

FIELD NOTES

As their name implies, Forbidden Root's credo is infusing various plants of all sorts into their beers. This may include wildflowers, gin botanicals, cacao, spices, and roots of all sorts. The brewery's mission statement is a throwback to American brewing history, when brewers would infuse their lower-ABV beverages with whatever flavoring and bittering agents they could find. Forbidden Root's aim is to bring back this sense of experimentation and marry it with a food menu that seeks to accentuate these botanical brews.

1746 W. Chicago Ave.
Chicago, IL 60622
312-929-2202
forbiddenroot.com

OWNER	**DATE FOUNDED**
Robert Finkel	2013
HEAD BREWER	**2016 PRODUCTION**
BJ Pichman	3,000 bbl
AVAILABILITY	**PUBLIC TRANSIT**
Chicago, FL, MA, OH	'L' Blue/Division
BEST KNOWN FOR	
Spiced/herbed ales, NE IPAs	

16 | 258 | | | | | • | | • | 4.0/5

FORBIDDEN ROOT

PRO TIPS

» Located in the hip East Village neighborhood, enjoy the local flavor with Chicago Avenue's array of cafés, record stores, and even a true-blue western-wear outfitter.

» Furnished with couches, tables for groups and a bar in the middle, the space invites everyone from those interested in dinner to casual drinks with friends.

» They call themselves Chicago's first botanical brewery. One hundred percent of their profits from non-consumable merchandise go to Green City Market.

» Reservations are recommended on weekend evenings.

DATE OF VISIT:

MY RATING
☆ ☆ ☆ ☆ ☆

NOTES:

POPULAR BEERS

M	Tu	W	Th	F	S	Su
11a-12a	11a-12a	11a-12a	11a-12a	11a-12a	11a-12a	11a-12a

GINO'S BREWING CO.

FIELD NOTES

500 N. LaSalle Dr.
Chicago, IL 60654
312-988-4200
**ginoseastrivernorth.
com/beer-wine/
beer/**

Gino's East is generally regarded as one of the main three progenitors of the Chicago-style deep dish pizza. For the uninitiated, Chicago-style deep dish is a massive, multi-layered creation that features a hearty, bready crust, a helping of cheese that would make any cardiologist or dairy farmer blush, and the tomato sauce on the top of the pie. It's a mandatory experience for the Chicago tourist. Around since 1966, Gino's East became the first of the big three Chicago pizza joints to open a brewery in one of their locations in 2015.

OWNER
Bravo Restaurants

HEAD BREWER
Kevin McMahon

AVAILABILITY
Gino's East
restaurants only

BEST KNOWN FOR
Session ales, pales

DATE FOUNDED
2015

2016 PRODUCTION
2,000 bbl

RECENT AWARDS
U.S. Open Beer Cup
2015

PUBLIC TRANSIT
'L' Red/Grand,
Brown/Merch. Mart

11 | 340 | • | | • | • | | • | | • | 3.6/5

GINO'S BREWING CO.

PRO TIPS

» Give yourself plenty of time at Gino's, as getting a table usually takes some patience, depending on the size of your party. Also, allow yourself time to enjoy a deep-dish pie; it goes a long way toward soaking up the beer.

» In its short history, Gino's has won an impressive number of awards, including several at the 2015 U.S. Open Beer Cup.

» The multi-level facility also features live music and a comedy club.

» Michael Jordan's Restaurant occupied the space from 1993 to 1999.

DATE OF VISIT:

MY RATING
☆ ☆ ☆ ☆ ☆

NOTES:

POPULAR BEERS

Broken English	Witte Chicks Dig Me	LaSalle Street	Pine-apple Imposter

M	Tu	W	Th	F	S	Su
11a-10p	11a-10p	11a-10p	11a-10p	11a-11p	11a-11p	11a-10p

GOOSE ISLAND BEER CO.

FIELD NOTES

1800 W. Fulton St.
Chicago, IL 60612
312-226-1119
gooseisland.com

Goose Island is, for all intents and purposes, the granddaddy of craft beer in Chicago. The longest-running brewery in Chicago, Goose Island began as a small brewpub in a then-run down industrial part of the Lincoln Park neighborhood. Founder John Hall returned from a European sojourn with a love for the continent's beer and the culture surrounding it. In 2015, Goose Island added a taproom to their production facility in the Fulton Market neighborhood. The taproom features some experimental and exclusive beers, as well as plenty of longtime favorites.

OWNER
AB InBev

HEAD BREWER
Jared Jankowski

AVAILABILITY
Nationwide

BEST KNOWN FOR
Pales, barrel-aged beers

DATE FOUNDED
1988

2016 PRODUCTION
N/A

KEY EVENTS
BCBS Release (Nov), 312 Block Party (Sept)

PUBLIC TRANSIT
'L' Green or Pink/ Ashland (Fulton)

16 | 100 | | | | | | | | | • | 3.9/5

GOOSE ISLAND BEER CO.

PRO TIPS

» The stylish and modern taproom has plenty of vintage bottles and Goose memorabilia for sale.

» The bar will get packed with the post-work crowd and on weekends, so retreat to one of several tables if you don't want folks shouting a beer order behind you.

» Rare beers will show up randomly on the draft list including Bourbon County Stout variants.

» Many Goose Island beers start out being only available at the taproom.

» The Clybourn brewpub (1800 N. Clybourn Ave.) is currently undergoing a massive renovation, and will be reopening later in 2017.

DATE OF VISIT:

MY RATING
☆ ☆ ☆ ☆ ☆

NOTES:

POPULAR BEERS

M	Tu	W	Th	F	S	Su
closed	closed	closed	2p-8p	2p-9p	12p-9p	12p-6p

HAYMARKET PUB & BREWERY

FIELD NOTES

Haymarket Square, on Chicago's near west side, is the site of, arguably, the birth of the American (and worldwide) labor movement. The "Haymarket Affair," as it is called, is the inspiration for many of the world's May Day celebrations for workers' rights. Now this area is home to a large portion of Chicago's blossoming culinary scene, including Haymarket. Brewer/Owner Pete Crowley got his start as the head brewer at Rock Bottom Chicago, leading into his own venture in 2010. His beers have won many awards over the years.

737 W. Randolph St.
Chicago, IL 60661
312-638-0700
**haymarketbrewing.
com**

Photo Credit: Gosia Photography

OWNER
John Neurauter,
Pete Crowley

HEAD BREWER
Pete Crowley

AVAILABILITY
Chicago, MI

BEST KNOWN FOR
IPAs, pales, Belgians

DATE FOUNDED
2010

2016 PRODUCTION
1,100 bbl

RECENT AWARDS
WBC 2016

KEY EVENTS
SausageFest (Feb)

PUBLIC TRANSIT
'L' Green or Pink/
Clinton

24 | 400 | • | | • | • | | • | | • | 3.7/5

HAYMARKET PUB & BREWERY

PRO TIPS

» The space is sizable, with a bar area and a dining room both ready to accommodate plenty.

» The back bar is home to Chicago's Drinking & Writing Theater.

» The food menu is fairly standard fare, pub grub done well. Expect sandwiches, pizzas, appetizers (try the sweet potato tots, they'll make you want an industrial-sized bag of them at home), and entrées. Brunch on weekends.

» Haymarket recently opened a production facility in Bridgman, MI, meant to expand distribution beyond the brewpub.

» Both bars feature plenty of TV's always tuned into the latest sporting events

Photo Credit: Gosia Photography

DATE OF VISIT:

MY RATING
☆ ☆ ☆ ☆ ☆

NOTES:

POPULAR BEERS

| Mathias Imperial IPA | The Defender | Aleister | Angry Birds |

M	Tu	W	Th	F	S	Su
11a-2a	11a-2a	11a-2a	11a-2a	11a-2a	11a-3a	11a-2a

LAGUNITAS BREWING COMPANY

FIELD NOTES

1843 S. Washtenaw Ave.
Chicago, IL 60608
773-522-1308
lagunitas.com

Lagunitas founder Tony Magee has admittedly always been a Chicago guy, though he started the brewery in his family's home in California. After building a sizable operation in Petaluma, Lagunitas expanded to this enormous facility on the south side of Chicago near Jackson Park. Housed in an old movie studio, Lagunitas got cheap rent under a 100-year lease on the unused space and have since turned it into the largest brewery in the city. In fact, combine all of the other breweries in the state of Illinois, and you still won't match their capacity.

OWNER Heineken	**DATE FOUNDED** 1993
HEAD BREWER Mary Bauer	**2016 PRODUCTION** N/A
AVAILABILITY Nationwide	**KEY EVENTS** Beer Circus (Sept)
BEST KNOWN FOR Everything hoppy	**PUBLIC TRANSIT** 'L' Pink/California

16	250			•		•	•	•	4.1/5

LAGUNITAS BREWING COMPANY

PRO TIPS

» Due to the sheer, massive size of the facility, the Lagunitas brewery tour is one not to miss. In addition to the free beer, the tour will take you up to the brewery's pub space and out onto the catwalks that traverse the space, giving you a bird's eye view of the brewing, packaging, and shipping operations that make a brewery of this scale hum. Tours will soon be reservable online.

» The tones of "Pure Imagination" from Willy Wonka and the Chocolate Factory will serenade you as you enter.

» A small food menu has snacks, shareables, and sandwiches, incorporating beer in someway.

» Live music is in the taproom most weekends.

POPULAR BEERS

M	Tu	W	Th	F	S	Su
closed	closed	12p-9p	12p-9p	12p-9p	12p-9p	12p-9p

DATE OF VISIT:

MY RATING

☆ ☆ ☆ ☆ ☆

NOTES:

MAD MOUSE BREWING

FIELD NOTES

724 W. Maxwell St.
Chicago, IL 60607
312-243-3660
**moxeerestaurant.
com/mad-mouse-
brewery/**

Mad Mouse is the brewery that partners with Moxee, a Cajun and barbecue restaurant that resides near the campus of the University of Illinois-Chicago (UIC). Special brews include a seasonal harvest ale that uses hops grown on the south side of the city, and their annual Devil Doll series of Belgian Golden Strong Ales. The brewery itself certainly qualifies as "nano" as opposed to "micro;" batches are only 1.5 barrels each, with styles gravitating more toward universally-liked, less-divisive styles.

OWNER
Rob Strom, Gavin Gillan

HEAD BREWER
Philip Zelewsky

AVAILABILITY
Brewpub only

BEST KNOWN FOR
Pales, IPAs, cream ales, Kölsch

DATE FOUNDED
2014

2016 PRODUCTION
N/A

24 | 205 | • | | • | • | | • | | 3.7/5

MAD MOUSE BREWING

PRO TIPS

» The Moxee facility is located in a gorgeous old building on Chicago's historical Maxwell Street. Maxwell was one of Chicago's first major residential districts, and used to be the home of a massive street market that took place every Sunday from the late 19th century until 1994. Maxwell Street was also one of the incubators of the Chicago blues sound.

» The Cajun-inspired food menu's options are robust, with Shrimp Creole, house-made andouille sausage, catfish and crawfish etoufée.

» Friday evenings will often feature a CHIRP DJ spinning tunes, and happy hour specials are available 4-6p Tuesday-Saturday.

» Table shuffleboard is available.

POPULAR BEERS

Rath-mandu	Schnick-elfritz	Hippie Johnny	Langer Mann

DATE OF VISIT:

MY RATING
☆ ☆ ☆ ☆ ☆

NOTES:

M	Tu	W	Th	F	S	Su
closed	11:30-1a	11:30-1a	11:30-1a	11:30-1a	11:30-1a	10a-10p

MOODY TONGUE BREWING COMPANY

FIELD NOTES

2136 S. Peoria St.
Chicago, IL 60608
312-600-5111
moodytongue.com

Chicago's reputation as a food and beer destination has led to people who began in one arena forging into careers in the other, which is how we get the food-infused and inspired beers of Moody Tongue. Head Brewer Jared Rouben is yet another Goose Island alum. He was head brewer at the Clybourn brewpub for several years before striking out on his own. Rouben's background is in the culinary industry, and he brings that expertise and passion for flavor into all his beers, balancing the notes and components of his food adjuncts while accentuating the beers themselves.

OWNER
Jared Rouben

HEAD BREWER
Jared Rouben

AVAILABILITY
Chicago, New York City, San Fran., Las Vegas, Shanghai, Toronto, Houston, AL, GA, KY

BEST KNOWN FOR
IPAs, saisons, food-infused beers

DATE FOUNDED
2014

2016 PRODUCTION
3,000 bbl

KEY EVENTS
Valentines Day Beer & Cake Pairing (Feb)

PUBLIC TRANSIT
'L' Orange/Halsted

12	95			•		•			•	•	4.0/5

MOODY TONGUE BREWING COMPANY

PRO TIPS

» Expect a luxurious sort of minimalism at the Moody Tongue tasting room. The feel is very modern, one of the more stylish brewpub spaces in the city.

» The food menu features only two items, fresh oysters and an endlessly-layered German chocolate cake, both designed to pair with Rouben's "chef-driven" beer options.

» On especially rare occasions, guests may try small pours of MT's Shaved Black Truffle Pilsner, a lighter-style lager made with rare mushrooms designed to highlight the savory character of the added ingredient.

» There's no sign for Moody Tongue so you'll have to look for the unmarked door on the east side of the building.

Photo Credit: Jordan Balderas

DATE OF VISIT:

MY RATING
☆ ☆ ☆ ☆ ☆

NOTES:

POPULAR BEERS

M	Tu	W	Th	F	S	Su
5p-10p	closed	closed	5p-11p	5p-12a	12p-12a	12p-9p

MOTOR ROW BREWING

FIELD NOTES

2337 S. Michigan Ave.
Chicago, IL 60616
312-624-8149
**motorrowbrewing.
com**

Head Brewer Frank Lassandrello is a Goose Island alum whose travels have brought him back to Chicago and Motor Row. Motor Row is located in the historical district that unofficially shares its name with this rather new brewery. A fine balance of lagers and ales has always been Lassandrello's specialty, and he continues that at Motor Row. Scores of auto-related manufacturers and dealers used to be housed on this stretch of Michigan Avenue, which also has a deep music history as Record Row (Chess Records, Vee-Jay Records and more).

OWNER
Bob Lassandrello

HEAD BREWER
Frank Lassandrello

AVAILABILITY
Chicago

BEST KNOWN FOR
Lagers, American ales

DATE FOUNDED
2015

2016 PRODUCTION
1,500 bbl

PUBLIC TRANSIT
'L' Red or Green/
Cermak-McCormick
Place

8   200 | | • | • | | • | | • | 4.0/5

MOTOR ROW BREWING

PRO TIPS

» Growlers available from the brewery are from Hydro Flask, which advertises technological advances in the storing and preservation of consumable liquids.

» Live blues jam every Thursday night.

» Expect to see a number of out-of-towners due to its proximity to the McCormick Place Convention Center.

» Motor Row will likely become a popular pregame destination for the Wintrust Arena, the new home of DePaul basketball for the 2017-18 season.

DATE OF VISIT:

MY RATING
☆ ☆ ☆ ☆ ☆

NOTES:

POPULAR BEERS

Out Of The Loop IPL	Recla-mation Lager	New Phenix Lager	Dry Humor Begian

M	Tu	W	Th	F	S	Su
4p-10p	4p-10p	4p-10p	4p-10p	12p-11p	12p-11p	2p-8p

ON TOUR BREWING CO.

FIELD NOTES

Newly opened in January 2017, On Tour is the brainchild of Mark Legenza. He started homebrewing in Denver in 2009 and moved back to Chicago in 2015 to open the music-themed On Tour. Head brewer Mark Poffenberger began his craft beer journey as employee #1 at Indianapolis' Sun King Brewing, and later brewing at Fat Head's brewpub in Portland. The goal of the brewery is to produce an approachable variety of beers meant for people to take a moment to "press pause and enjoy."

1725 W. Hubbard St.
Chicago, IL 60622
312-796-3119
**ontourbrewingco.
com**

Photo Credit: Vanessa Buholzer

OWNER
Mark Legenza

HEAD BREWER
Mark Poffenberger

AVAILABILITY
Chicago - limited
draft only

BEST KNOWN FOR
IPAs, British styles

DATE FOUNDED
2017

2016 PRODUCTION
N/A

PUBLIC TRANSIT
'L' Green/Ashland

| 12 | 98 | | | • | • | | | | • | 4.4/5 |

ON TOUR BREWING CO.

PRO TIPS

» On Tour offers a bimonthly yoga series cleverly called "Om Tour."

» Arigato Taco has a pop-up shop Thursday and Friday evenings, as well as Saturdays and Sundays during the lunchtime hour.

» On Tour is not far from United Center in case you want to catch a Blackhawks or Bulls game.

» The space is bright and vibrant, with a big glass window behind the bar opening into the brewhouse.

» Credit card only.

» Hours may be different in the winter months, so check the website ahead of a planned visit.

Photo Credit: Vanessa Buholzer

DATE OF VISIT:

MY RATING
☆ ☆ ☆ ☆ ☆

NOTES:

POPULAR BEERS

| It Takes Two | Wake Me Up Before You Go-Go | Silly Grin | Paradise Waits |

M	Tu	W	Th	F	S	Su
closed	3p-10p	3p-10p	3p-10p	2p-11p	11a-11p	11a-8p

VICE DISTRICT BREWING CO.

FIELD NOTES

1454 S. Michigan Ave.
Chicago, IL 60605
312-291-9022
**vicedistrictbrewing.
com**

South Side Chicago natives Quintin Cole and Curtis Tarver II unknowingly put themselves on the road to starting Vice District Brewing when they bought homes across the street from one another. In what sounds like a sitcom plot, the two were soon homebrewing together, hosting beer gatherings, and ultimately deciding to start their own venture in the South Loop neighborhood. Cole and Tarver's plan is to be that gathering place where people can enter as guests but leave as friends.

OWNER
Curtis Tarver II,
Quintin Cole

HEAD BREWER
Aydan Connor

AVAILABILITY
Taproom only

BEST KNOWN FOR
IPAs, American
takes on English
styles

DATE FOUNDED
2013

2016 PRODUCTION
800 bbl

PUBLIC TRANSIT
'L' Red, Green or
Orange/Roosevelt

16 | 99 | | | • | | • | | • | | | | | • | 3.8/5

VICE DISTRICT BREWING CO.

PRO TIPS

» Lots of bar seating and beer-hall style tables, with windows that open wide on warm days.

» Beers are British-inspired for the most part, with some Belgian and German interjections.

» Regularly hosted events seem to have a fitness theme. Wednesdays are the meetings of the Vice District Run Club and every other Saturday afternoon features body workout classes like Pure Barre or Vinyasa. Check their website calendar for details.

» A second location with a production facility and taproom is currently in the works for downtown Homewood in the south suburbs.

» Board games are available.

DATE OF VISIT:

MY RATING

NOTES:

POPULAR BEERS

M	Tu	W	Th	F	S	Su
closed	4p-11p	4p-11p	4p-11p	4p-1a	2p-1a	2p-9p

1. Horse Thief Hollow
   Brewing Co.
2. Whiner Beer Co.

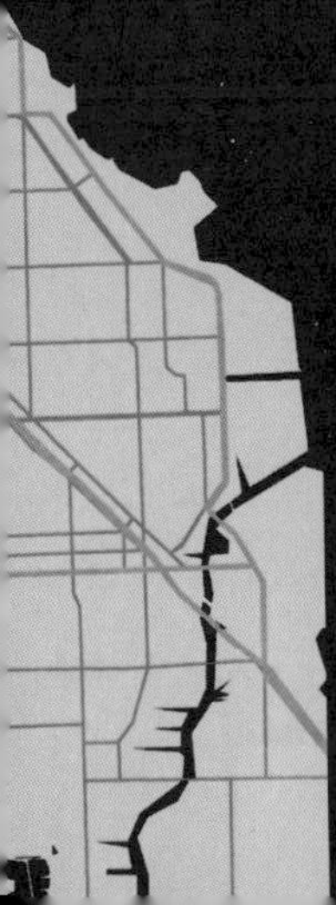

NEIGHBORHOOD HIGHLIGHTS

1 Guaranteed Rate
  Field

2 The Pullman State
  Historic Site

3 The Original
  Rainbow Cone

HORSE THIEF HOLLOW BREWING CO.

FIELD NOTES

10426 S. Western Ave.
Chicago, IL 60643
773-779-2739
**horsethiefbrewing.
com**

Located on the far south side in the Beverly neighborhood, Horse Thief Hollow is still worth the time to get there. In a space that used to be occupied by a carpet store, Horse Thief Hollow has established itself as a vital cultural outpost for the community. After working for almost a decade as a chef in Charleston, SC, Neil Byers enlisted help from his entire family in renovating Horse Thief Hollow's current space, even using reclaimed carved-wood doors for the building's entrance. The beers and food are given just as much care as their surroundings.

OWNER
Neil Byers

HEAD BREWER
David Williams

AVAILABILITY
Chicago - limited

BEST KNOWN FOR
Pales, IPAs, stouts, Kölsch

DATE FOUNDED
2013

2016 PRODUCTION
N/A

RECENT AWARDS
GABF 2016, FoBAB 2016

PUBLIC TRANSIT
RI/103rd St.-Beverly Hills

| 12 | 160 | | | • | • | | | • | • | • | 3.8/5 |

HORSE THIEF HOLLOW BREWING CO.

PRO TIPS

- » The food menu, as Byers' history might indicate, is resplendently Southern-inspired with BBQ, Nashville Hot Frog Legs and crab cakes. However, there are few places in town that offer Rocky Mountain Oysters (beef testicles, a true delicacy) on their menu.
- » Monthly live music shows and Art on Tap, a series showcasing the work of local artists.
- » Chicago Magazine named it one of the top 50 bars in Chicago.
- » If you make the trip to Horse Thief Hollow, you must also visit the legendary Original Rainbow Cone (in season).
- » The too-new-to-review Open Outcry Brewing Co. is less than a mile south.

DATE OF VISIT:

MY RATING
☆ ☆ ☆ ☆ ☆

NOTES:

POPULAR BEERS

Annexation Ale	Kitchen Sink Pale Ale	Ridge Rider	18th Rebellion

M	Tu	W	Th	F	S	Su
11:30-10	11:30-10	11:30-10	11:30-10	11:30-12	11:30-12	11:30-10

WHINER BEER CO.

FIELD NOTES

1400 W. 46th St.
Chicago, IL 60609
312-810-2271
whinerbeer.com

Whiner is, like a few Chicago breweries, a bit of a refreshing anomaly. There are no IPA's and the taproom isn't located in a heavily-trafficked neighborhood. That said, head brewer Brian Taylor, a Goose Island alum, is brewing an impressive array of wild and barrel-aged beers while Ria Neri, who's developed beer programs for several Chicago restaurants, is focusing on the business side. The beers all have a hint of sourness to them, but that doesn't mean they're unapproachable.

OWNER
Brian Taylor, Ria Neri

HEAD BREWER
Brian Taylor

AVAILABILITY
Chicago

BEST KNOWN FOR
Sours, lighter
Belgians

DATE FOUNDED
2016

2016 PRODUCTION
N/A

| 10 | 100 | | | • | • | | | | • | | 4.1/5 |

WHINER BEER CO.

PRO TIPS

» Whiner is located in The Plant, an incredibly unique sustainable business project, with a fish farm, farmers' market and other businesses designed to use each other's resources to create a net-zero energy facility. There's nothing else like it in the city.

» Barrel-aged beers are sometimes available in bottles to go.

» Tours of The Plant are available; book ahead on their website.

» There are no bum picks on the growing tap list, including a modest number of Belgian and French-inspired ales with an accent on adjuncts (i.e., apple-infused Kölsch).

DATE OF VISIT:

MY RATING
☆ ☆ ☆ ☆ ☆

NOTES:

POPULAR BEERS

M	Tu	W	Th	F	S	Su
closed	closed	closed	2p-10p	2p-10p	11a-10p	1p-8p

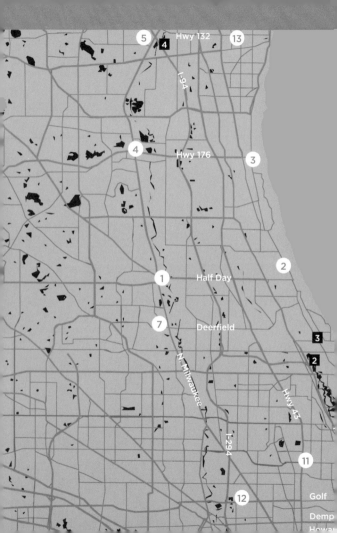

SUBURBS NORTH

NEIGHBORHOOD HIGHLIGHTS

HALF DAY BREWING

FIELD NOTES

Half Day is named after the Chief of the Potawatomi tribe that helped non-native Americans first settle in the area. Right off the highway, this Native American themed brewpub offers something for everyone. The brewpub is very large, able to accommodate groups of just about any size. In the summer, they also have a large patio with a beautiful fountain that allows for soaking up the sun while drinking. Note that only a few of the 40 taps are dedicated to their own beer, but they also offer a full bar, wide guest beer selection and a full menu for your hunger needs.

200 Village Green
Lincolnshire, IL
60069
847-821-6933
halfdaybrewing.com

OWNER
Scott Ward, Mark Zych

HEAD BREWER
Brandon Boshers

AVAILABILITY
Brewpub only

BEST KNOWN FOR
IPAs, dark ales

DATE FOUNDED
2015

2016 PRODUCTION
300 bbl

40 | 400 | • | | • | • | | • | • | | 3.5/5

HALF DAY BREWING

PRO TIPS

- » TVs dot just about every wall, making this the perfect place to watch your favorite sports teams.
- » Chicken wings are award-winning.
- » Cozy up to the fireplace during Chicago's long winter months.
- » It can get a bit loud around the bar area, but other dining areas do offer a softer tone.
- » The patio option is second to none, with fire pits and a fountain.
- » The weekend brunch is very popular.
- » Can host private events for up to 400 people.

DATE OF VISIT:

MY RATING
☆ ☆ ☆ ☆ ☆

NOTES:

POPULAR BEERS

Full Day IPA	Chieftain Session IPA	Iron Horse Porter	Wet Hop Black RyePA

M	Tu	W	Th	F	S	Su
11a-12a	11a-12a	11a-12a	11a-12a	11a-1a	11a-1a	11a-10p

KINGS & CONVICTS BREWING CO.

FIELD NOTES

Something magical happens when you bring together a Brit, an Aussie and a passion for beer - you get Kings & Convicts Brewing. Opened only a few weeks before publication of this field guide, these guys have found the right combination of experience and creativity that has allowed them to jump out of the starting gates strong. Chris honed his skills in the chemistry and technology segment, while co-owner Brenden earned his stripes in the hospitality industry. With both a pilot and a 15 barrel brew system in house, expect to see special things to come from this duo.

523 Bank Lane
Highwood, IL 60040
224-707-0117
kingsandconvicts. com

OWNER
Chris Bradley,
Brendan Waters

HEAD BREWER
Chris Bradley

AVAILABILITY
Chicago - very
limited

BEST KNOWN FOR
British-style pales
and IPAs, pilsners

DATE FOUNDED
2017

2016 PRODUCTION
N/A

PUBLIC TRANSIT
UP-N/Highwood

| 8 | 30 | • | • | • | | | | | • | • | NA/5 |

KINGS & CONVICTS BREWING CO.

PRO TIPS

» The taproom is very small and intimate, but a large patio area adds seating and is great for summer.

» There's no actual bar seating as the entire counter is for ordering only.

» Board games are scattered around the tables for those who need something more than beer to pass the time.

» The background Motown and classic rock music doesn't interfere with conversation between tables.

» Lack auto transportation? No worries as this taproom is steps from the Highwood Metra station.

» Their most popular beers tend towards a malt forward balance, versus enamel peeling hop notes.

» Pre-filled crowler to-go cans available.

DATE OF VISIT:

MY RATING
☆ ☆ ☆ ☆ ☆

NOTES:

POPULAR BEERS

M	Tu	W	Th	F	S	Su
closed	4p-9p	4p-9p	4p-9p	4p-10p	12p-10p	4:30-9

LAKE BLUFF BREWING CO.

FIELD NOTES

In 2010, the very charming Village of Lake Bluff on Chicago's North Shore finally got its own brewery. It sits on a quaint village shopping area across the street from a wooded park, perfect for sidewalk sipping during the summer months. Lake Bluff organizes their beer menu in order of intensity, allowing pour sizes of 4, 10 and 16 ounces. While exploring their wide variety of beer, make sure to enjoy the local art carefully displayed throughout the newly remodeled space.

16 E. Scranton Ave.
Lake Bluff, IL 60044
224-544-5179
lbbrew.com

OWNER
Mike Dorneker

HEAD BREWER
Mike Dorneker

AVAILABILITY
Chicago

BEST KNOWN FOR
Imperial stouts,
blonde ales, IPAs

DATE FOUNDED
2010

2016 PRODUCTION
300 bbl

RECENT AWARDS
FoBAB 2016

PUBLIC TRANSIT
UP-N/Lake Bluff

| 14 | 60 | • | • | • | | | • | • | 3.8/5 |

LAKE BLUFF BREWING CO.

PRO TIPS

» Dog friendly on the patio only.

» While food is not prepared on site, you can easily order food from the Maevery Public House next door and have it delivered right to your table.

» They are planning on bottling beer in the fall of 2017 by expanding production to Octopi Brewing in Wisconsin.

» Watch for great summer block parties.

» The Metra drops you off only steps from the brewery's front door.

DATE OF VISIT:

» Load up your bikes and take advantage of the numerous bike trails around this tranquil community.

MY RATING
☆ ☆ ☆ ☆ ☆

» Frequent live music and beer and cupcakes pairings.

NOTES:

POPULAR BEERS

Inspiration Pale Ale	Skull And Bones	Velvet Hammer Vanilla Porter	Honey Badger

M	Tu	W	Th	F	S	Su
closed	5p-10p	5p-10p	5p-11p	12p-12a	12p-12a	12p-6p

MICKEY FINN'S BREWERY

FIELD NOTES

345 N. Milwaukee Ave.
Libertyville, IL 60048
847-362-6688
**mickeyfinnsbrewery.
com**

Mickey Finn's has been around since 1993 as a brewery, and as a restaurant for even longer than that. Operating out of the northern suburb of Libertyville, Finn's lays the claim of being Lake County's first brewpub. Catering to its fans, as well as its surrounding suburban audience, Mickey Finn's hits the middle ground between heavy and lighter styles. For every Orange Is the New Chocolate barrel-aged orange zest and chocolate stout, there's an 847 Suburban Wheat Ale (a mild dig, no doubt, at a certain Chicago brewery's Urban Wheat Ale).

OWNER
Brian Grano, Jetta Grano

HEAD BREWER
Greg Browne

AVAILABILITY
Brewpub only

BEST KNOWN FOR
IPAs, classic American styles

DATE FOUNDED
1993

2016 PRODUCTION
1,100 bbl

KEY EVENTS
St. Paddy's Day (Mar), Get Lit (Nov)

PUBLIC TRANSIT
MD-N/Libertyville

16 | 300 | • | | | • | | • | • | • | 3.6/5

MICKEY FINN'S BREWERY

PRO TIPS

» The exposed brick and thoughtful lighting of the interior give a modern look to a business that's been around for a couple decades.

» There's a long bar offering decent seating and lots of TVs for sports watching.

» The food menu is fairly standard suburban pub fare (pizzas, burgers, spinach and artichoke dip, etc.).

» 2-for-1 burgers every Wednesday and a $4 pint of the day every Thursday.

» Live music is a feature on weekends, ranging from country to blues, but check in advance to see who is playing.

DATE OF VISIT:

MY RATING

NOTES:

POPULAR BEERS

| Pine-apple Express | Santa's Magic | Amber Ale |

M	Tu	W	Th	F	S	Su
11-11:30	11-11:30	11-11:30	11-11:30	11a-1:15	11a-1:15	11a-9p

ONLY CHILD BREWING

FIELD NOTES

1350 Tri State Pkwy
Gurnee, IL 60031
224-656-5241
**onlychildbrewing.
com**

Ben and Amanda Rossi are the husband
and wife team behind Only Child,
situated near the Wisconsin border.
Originally based out of Northbrook,
Only Child's move to Gurnee offers the
Rossi's an expansion in production, as
well as taproom space. Like many other
smaller operations dotting the suburban
Chicago brewing landscape, the charm
in Only Child is their ability to create a
brewery and taproom out of what would
otherwise be a lifeless industrial concrete
space, injecting it with a passion and
determination found in their creations.

OWNER
Benjamin Rossi,
Amanda Rossi

HEAD BREWER
Benjamin Rossi

AVAILABILITY
Chicago - mostly
Lake County

BEST KNOWN FOR
IPAs, saisons

DATE FOUNDED
2013

2016 PRODUCTION
500 bbl

KEY EVENTS
Anniversary
Celebration (Aug)

8 | 50 | • | • | • | • | • | | • | | 4.1/5

ONLY CHILD BREWING

PRO TIPS

» The space is rather narrow and long, so what the Only Child folks have done is split the tasting room space in two by placing the bar in the middle, essentially creating separate spaces, one closer to the door with tables, and the other closer to the brewery with barrels.

» Package releases are periodical and tend to oscillate between cans and bottles, and are sometimes cash only. Releases always sell out, so plan accordingly.

» Live music on summer Friday nights.

» Gurnee is also home to Six Flags Great America, the nearest major amusement park to Chicago.

DATE OF VISIT:

MY RATING
☆ ☆ ☆ ☆ ☆

NOTES:

POPULAR BEERS

M	Tu	W	Th	F	S	Su
4p-9p	4p-9p	4p-9p	4p-9p	11a-11p	11a-11p	12p-7p

PECKISH PIG

FIELD NOTES

Advertising itself as Evanston's first brewpub (which is true, since Temperance and Sketchbook don't have their own kitchens), Peckish Pig opened up just on the other side of the Chicago border in 2014. The space was previously used to house a dry cleaner, a nail salon, and a record store (a nice revitalization of the street). Owner Debbie Evans is originally from Liverpool and has made Peckish Pig quite the family affair, with children India and Janek both getting into the act, as well.

623 Howard St.
Evanston, IL 60202
847-491-6778
thepeckishpig.com

OWNER
Debbie Evans

HEAD BREWER
Tom Fogarty

AVAILABILITY
Brewpub only

BEST KNOWN FOR
IPAs, Belgians, British styles

DATE FOUNDED
2014

2016 PRODUCTION
350 bbl

PUBLIC TRANSIT
'L' Red, Purple or Yellow/Howard

| 12 | 180 | • | | • | • | | • | | • | 3.7/5 |

PECKISH PIG

PRO TIPS

» There's a decent-sized wine list, a small cocktail list, guest beers and well-curated whiskey list.

» Peckish Pig has a large, stylish patio available during the summer months.

» The food menu is hearty, British-style pub fare. Sausage rolls, rabbit, boar tacos, fish and chips, lamb kebabs, Moroccan cassoulet, and bone marrow.

» The bacon-wrapped dates are to die for.

» Note that on weekends, the kitchen closes from 3:30p-4:30p to allow for the switch from brunch to dinner service.

» Trivia nights on Tuesdays and old school dance parties every month.

DATE OF VISIT:

MY RATING
☆ ☆ ☆ ☆ ☆

NOTES:

POPULAR BEERS

India's Panic Attack	George Mahal	Bigger Baby	Live Free Or Rye Hard

M	Tu	W	Th	F	S	Su
closed	4p-10p	4p-10p	4p-10p	4p-12a	11a-12a	11a-10p

PRAIRIE KRAFTS BREWING COMPANY

FIELD NOTES

Mannish Khosla founded Prairie Krafts in order to bring craft beer to the northwestern suburb of Buffalo Grove. Khosla and co-owner Raj Chauhan provide a friendly, neighborhood vibe to the town's first brewery, offering plenty of gateway beers, and a couple of heavy hitters for those willing to jump into the deep end of the pool. Prairie Krafts does not currently package beers, but drafts are available all over the northern suburbs, and some kegs are even creeping their way into the city if you want to look hard enough.

1310 Busch Pkwy
Buffalo Grove, IL
60089
224-434-2189
prairiekrafts.com

OWNER
Mannish Khosla, Raj Chauhan

HEAD BREWER
Matt Lakota,
Mannish Khosla, Raj Chauhan

AVAILABILITY
Chicago - draft only

BEST KNOWN FOR
Variety

DATE FOUNDED
2016

2016 PRODUCTION
700 bbl

KEY EVENTS
Anniversary Party (Apr)

PUBLIC TRANSIT
NCS/Buffalo Grove

12 | 55 | | • | • | • | • | • | | • | • | 3.9/5

PRAIRIE KRAFTS BREWING COMPANY

PRO TIPS

» Prairie Krafts is located in an unassuming industrial park in the suburbs of Chicago. You will most likely drive by it your first time.

» Food trucks will only come by occasionally, so plan your eating schedule accordingly. That said, cookies made with spent grain from the brewery make frequent appearances. Try the spicy peanuts.

» Live music will be around every now and then, and even some open mic nights if you feel like bringing your own instrument.

» Features its own Mug Club for frequent customers.

DATE OF VISIT:

MY RATING

NOTES:

POPULAR BEERS

M	Tu	W	Th	F	S	Su
4p-9p	4p-9p	4p-9p	4p-9p	2p-11p	2p-11p	2p-7p

SKETCHBOOK BREWING COMPANY

FIELD NOTES

Clark Street in Chicago becomes Chicago Avenue in Evanston, and about a mile north of the border, right off the Main Street train stop is Sketchbook Brewing. Sketchbook is a tiny space that packs a lot of character into its small taproom. Much of the wood in the taproom is re-purposed, from the slats that cover the walls, to the re-purposed bowling alleys that cover the tables and bar top. Local artists also provide the neon lights and door murals on display. You can get the feeling that you're in a sort of modern day, craft beer speakeasy.

825 Chicago Ave.
Evanston, IL 60202
847-859-9051
**sketchbookbrewing.
com**

OWNER
Shawn Decker,
Cesar Marron,
Alice George, Amy
Wilkinson

HEAD BREWER
Cesar Marron

AVAILABILITY
Chicago

BEST KNOWN FOR
Pales, IPAs, Belgian
abbey, stouts

DATE FOUNDED
2014

2016 PRODUCTION
1,126 bbl

KEY EVENTS
Anniversary Party
(Apr), Custer Fair
(Jun)

PUBLIC TRANSIT
'L' Purple/Main,
UP-N/Main

| 12 | 45 | | | • | | | | | • | 4.0/5 |

SKETCHBOOK BREWING COMPANY

PRO TIPS

» Bring your own food, no kitchen. Packaged bar snacks are available.

» Bombers and 4-packs to go are regularly available.

» Features a CSB (community-supported brewery) program that features 1-2 regular growler fills for 6- or 12-month periods, other discounts, and invites to special events.

» Tours aren't frequent (2nd Saturday of each month), but are quite intimate, considering how small the space is.

» Located in Evanston, a walk around Northwestern's campus is a great activity after you're done drinking.

DATE OF VISIT:

MY RATING
☆ ☆ ☆ ☆ ☆

NOTES:

POPULAR BEERS

Orange Door	Snowy Owl	Back Alley Abbey	Night Game

M	Tu	W	Th	F	S	Su
closed	12p-10p	12p-10p	12p-10p	12p-11p	12p-11p	12p-8p

SMYLIE BROTHERS BREWING CO.

FIELD NOTES

SMYLIE
— brothers —
BREWING Cº

1615 Oak St.
Evanston, IL 60201
224-999-7320
smyliebros.com

Owner and founder Mike Smylie went from commodities trading to the culinary world to founding this charming brewpub just north of the city of Chicago in Evanston. Smylie Brothers marries Texas-style BBQ with well-considered house-made beers. Pizza and sandwiches are also available on the food front. The main dining area features two decent-sized bars, plenty of 4-top tables, and a few booths for families. Dutch-style bikes adorn the wall above the larger of the two bars and you can get a peek at the brewing setup itself from about any seat.

OWNER
Smylie Family

HEAD BREWER
Brad Pulver

AVAILABILITY
Brewpub only

BEST KNOWN FOR
CA Common, saisons, German wheats

DATE FOUNDED
2014

2016 PRODUCTION
1,300 bbl

RECENT AWARDS
GABF 2015, FoBAB 2016

PUBLIC TRANSIT
'L' Purple/Davis, UP-N/Davis

16 | 290 | • | • | • | • | • | • | • | 3.6/5

SMYLIE BROTHERS BREWING CO.

PRO TIPS

» Dog friendly on the patio only.

» In the process of converting the City of Evanston's former recycling center into a production facility for both draft and packaged beer.

» Upstairs mezzanine level features leather chairs and a private golf club sort of atmosphere.

» Reservations are not only available for seating, but also available for indoor parking two blocks away through ParqEx (use SMYLIE promo code).

» Happy hour Tuesday to Thursday and Sunday from 4-6p. There are several drink and food specials to choose from.

DATE OF VISIT:

MY RATING
☆ ☆ ☆ ☆ ☆

NOTES:

POPULAR BEERS

| Smylie Farm-house | Cali Common | Purple Line | Smylie Pale Ale |

M	Tu	W	Th	F	S	Su
closed	11-10:30	11-10:30	11-10:30	11-10:30	11-11:30	11-10:30

TEMPERANCE BEER CO.

FIELD NOTES

Evanston used to be a primary location for the Women's Christian Temperance Union, one of the largest lobbying groups that led the temperance movement in the early 1900's. Even after the repeal of prohibition in 1933, the WCTU still maintains its headquarters in Evanston. Evanston itself was dry until 1972, so shouting out the city's unique history with booze was an easy choice for the city's first brewery. Temperance features English and Belgian-inspired ales that provide unique twists on the classics.

2000 Dempster St.
Evanston, IL 60202
847-864-1000
**temperancebeer.
com**

Photo Credit: Genie Lemieux

OWNER
Josh Gilbert

HEAD BREWER
Jordan Binder,
Dave Gibbons, Mike
VanCamp

AVAILABILITY
Chicago

BEST KNOWN FOR
American take on
English styles

DATE FOUNDED
2013

2016 PRODUCTION
3,133 bbl

RECENT AWARDS
GABF 2016

KEY EVENTS
Greenwood Beach
Day (May), Might
Meets Right Release
(Winter)

12 | 300 | • | | • | | • | | • | | 4.0/5

TEMPERANCE BEER CO.

PRO TIPS

» Temperance is a great place to visit during warm weather. The large garage-style door on the front of the taproom will open up to the outside and let plenty of breeze and sunshine in. Patio seating is also available.

» Play some table shuffleboard; usually gets occupied quickly.

» Yoga on the third Saturday of the month at 1p. DJ events on Fridays during the summer.

» Food trucks featured on Fridays and Sundays. Bar snacks and cheese plates are also available.

» Kid-friendly until 8p.

POPULAR BEERS

GATECRASHER

RESTLESS YEARS

Escapist

MIGHT MEETS RIGHT

DATE OF VISIT:

MY RATING
☆ ☆ ☆ ☆ ☆

NOTES:

M	Tu	W	Th	F	S	Su
closed	closed	closed	4p-10p	4p-11p	12p-11p	12p-6p

TEN NINETY

1025 Waukegan Rd.
Glenview, IL 60025
224-432-5472
ten-ninety.com

Originally this suburban brewery only featured super-big, imperial-style beers. In fact their name, Ten Ninety, refers to the high original gravity (fermentable sugar concentration) of many of their original recipes. Soon after their launch, though, Ten Ninety began branching out into lower-ABV creations. Andy, Jamie, and Brian are the main men behind Ten Ninety, all having jettisoned from their jobs requiring far more advanced degrees. They originally brewed out of the Wisconsin border town of Zion, IL, before settling into their current home in Glenview, far closer to Chicago proper.

OWNER
Brian Schafer, Jamie Hoban, Andy Smith

HEAD BREWER
Gibbs Lippai

AVAILABILITY
Chicago

BEST KNOWN FOR
Imperial ales, IPAs, witbiers

DATE FOUNDED
2013

2016 PRODUCTION
N/A

PUBLIC TRANSIT
MD-N/Glenview

| 20 | 91 | · | · | · | ∞ | | | | MENU | P | | · | · | 3.7/5 |

TEN NINETY

PRO TIPS

- » Dog friendly on the patio only.
- » There is no kitchen, so feel free to bring your own food, though food trucks will come by occasionally.
- » The outside looks like a well-kept British-style pub, while the inside features a fireplace, overstuffed chairs, and a large, resplendent bar with friendly and educated staff.
- » There is ample bike parking and outdoor seating for days with nicer weather.
- » They occasionally have live music.
- » Most of their taps are dedicated to beer that isn't distributed or available anywhere else.

DATE OF VISIT:

MY RATING
☆ ☆ ☆ ☆ ☆

NOTES:

POPULAR BEERS

M	Tu	W	Th	F	S	Su
closed	closed	4p-10p	4p-10p	4p-10p	12p-10p	12p-8p

UNE ANNÉE/HUBBARD'S CAVE

FIELD NOTES

UNE ANNÉE

9082 W. Golf Rd.
Niles, IL 60714
847-635-0655
uneannee.com

Jerry Nelson's passion for brewing began while in the Marines in 1995. He attended the Siebel Institute, and, after leaving the architecture profession, started up the blueprints for what became Une Année (French for "one year") in 2013. After brewing for a couple years near Goose Island Fulton on the near west side of Chicago, Nelson found a more suitable space in the northwest suburb of Niles. Nelson spearheads both the Une Année line of French and Belgian-inspired ales, and the Hubbard's Cave brand of super-fresh IPAs and flavor-infused stouts.

OWNER Jerry Nelson	**DATE FOUNDED** 2013
HEAD BREWER Jerry Nelson	**2016 PRODUCTION** 713 bbl
AVAILABILITY IL, MI, MO, WI, Philadelphia	**KEY EVENTS** Monthly member- only releases
BEST KNOWN FOR Belgians, sours, Imperial IPAs	

| 12 | 45 | • | • | • | • | • | • | | • | | 4.3/5 |

UNE ANNÉE/HUBBARD'S CAVE

PRO TIPS

» Credit card only.

» The signage out front simply states "BREWERY," barely doing justice to the biological alchemy happening inside.

» The 24-hour Omega diner and bakery is in the same complex in a stand-alone space, and is a lovely little slice of Americana for the peckish insomniac.

» Le Grand Monde is not just a series of taproom beers, but also Une Année's CSA-inspired program. Allows subscribers to prepay to reserve bottles of Nelson's experimental barrel-aged sour beers, plus bottles of a couple other beers, a taproom discount, and a t-shirt.

DATE OF VISIT:

MY RATING
☆ ☆ ☆ ☆ ☆

NOTES:

POPULAR BEERS

① ① **HUBBARD'S CAVE VANILLA IMPERIAL STOUT** **HUBBARD'S CAVE IPA**

M	Tu	W	Th	F	S	Su
closed	closed	closed	4p-10p	4p-10p	12p-10p	12p-6p

ZÜMBIER

FIELD NOTES

ZümBier has been brewing out of the North Shore suburb of Waukegan since 2012, where it's been the labor of love of founder Larry Bloom and his wife Talea. Bloom's journey to craft beer began when the former whiskey drinker was handed a homebrew from his brother. That homebrew, a black rye double IPA, later become ZümBier's own Unda Cova Brudda. That moment of inspiration led Larry and Talea to pursue the idea of opening their own operation, which has culminated in ZümBier.

3232 Monroe
Waukegan, IL 60085
847-420-7313
zumbier.com

OWNER
Larry Bloom, Talea Bloom

HEAD BREWER
Larry Bloom

AVAILABILITY
Near Waukegan

BEST KNOWN FOR
Pales, IPAs, stouts, imperial styles

DATE FOUNDED
2012

2016 PRODUCTION
400 bbl

KEY EVENTS
Maui Trickster Release (Spring)

| 13 | 30 | • | • | • | • | | | | | • | | 4.2/5 |

ZÜMBIER

PRO TIPS

» ZümBier is housed in a large aquamarine-colored building that would be hard to mistake, even from a great distance.

» Lauren, a barrel-aged imperial porter, is not the only beer worthy of a marquee bottle release. Maui Trickster, a chocolate coconut milk stout with several variants, recently saw lots of attention for its first release party.

» The taproom itself is small, with a few barstools, tables and booths.

» They still brew on a 1.5 barrel system, so one-off beers can vanish quickly. But expect these guys to grow; they have plenty of room for expansion.

» Trivia on Thursday nights at 6:30p.

DATE OF VISIT:

MY RATING
☆ ☆ ☆ ☆ ☆

NOTES:

POPULAR BEERS

| Citra-Tasm | Lauren | Maui Trickster | Super Chong |

M	Tu	W	Th	F	S	Su
closed	closed	4p-9p	4p-9p	3p-10p	2p-10p	1p-6p

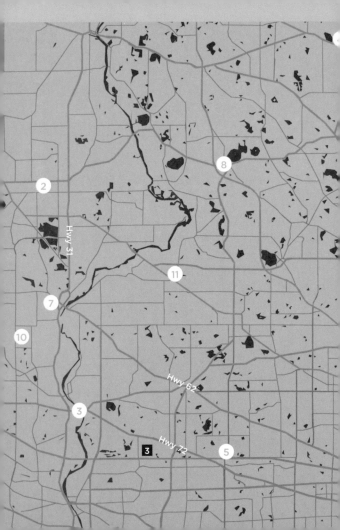

SUBURBS NORTHWEST

1. Bosacki's Home Brew
2. Crystal Lake Brewing
3. Emmett's Brewing Co.
4. Light The Lamp Brewery
5. The Lucky Monk
6. Mikerphone Brewing
7. Scorched Earth Brewing Company
8. Side Lot Brewery
9. Tighthead Brewing Company
10. Village Vintner Winery & Brewery
11. Wild Onion Brewery

NEIGHBORHOOD HIGHLIGHTS

1 O'Hare Int'l Airport
2 Arlington Int'l Racecourse
3 Sears Centre Arena
4 Independence Grove Forest Preserve

BOSACKI'S HOME BREW

FIELD NOTES

610 E. Hawley St.
Mundelein, IL 60060
224-778-5400
**bosackishomebrew.
com**

Named after owner Greg Bosacki, he and his wife Brigitte decided to take his homebrewing hobby to the next level in 2015. While beer can be consumed on premise, the space and mission still lean towards taking beer home to enjoy. Focusing on traditional styles featuring wheat ales, they have both year round beers along with many seasonal options. In addition to their passion for beer, they have great dedication to their local community, hosting events and fundraisers for multiple organizations around Mundelein.

OWNER
Greg Bosacki,
Brigitte Bosacki

HEAD BREWER
Greg Bosacki

AVAILABILITY
Taproom only

BEST KNOWN FOR
Sessionable
American styles,
German wheat ales

DATE FOUNDED
2015

2016 PRODUCTION
N/A

PUBLIC TRANSIT
NCS/Mundelein

| 12 | 69 | | | • | • | • | | • | • | 4.1/5 |

BOSACKI'S HOME BREW

PRO TIPS

» Wednesdays are $1 off pints.

» While snacks are limited to the free popcorn available, bringing your own food is always an option.

» Greg himself is usually tending bar; ask him to help you complete one of the many puzzles available.

» Occasionally, they invite guest brewers (home brewers) to share their recipes.

DATE OF VISIT:

MY RATING
☆ ☆ ☆ ☆ ☆

NOTES:

POPULAR BEERS

Back Porch Porter	I Wish Red Ale	Base- ment Bavarian Wheat	Word To The Weizen- bock

M	Tu	W	Th	F	S	Su
closed	closed	4p-9p	4p-9p	3p-10p	2p-10p	2p-6p

CRYSTAL LAKE BREWING

FIELD NOTES

150 N. Main St.
Crystal Lake, IL
60014
779-220-9288
**crystallakebrew.
com**

The town of Crystal Lake abuts Crystal Lake itself, as well as the Three Oaks Recreational Area, so you can bet that rest and relaxation are things that Crystal Lake Brewing takes seriously. You can imagine drinking these beers while boating or lazing on an inner tube. The life-preserver imagery on their cans goes hand-in-hand with their mantra of "beer that is easy to drink, and hard to put down." Their brewing philosophy is serious, though, with German ingredients imported for their blonde lager and plenty of care given to their Boathouse series of rare and barrel-aged beers.

OWNER
Chuck Ross, John O'Fallon

HEAD BREWER
Ryan Clooney

AVAILABILITY
Chicago

BEST KNOWN FOR
Session ales, IPAs, pale ales

DATE FOUNDED
2014

2016 PRODUCTION
2,500 bbl

RECENT AWARDS
WBC 2016

KEY EVENTS
Maibock Festival (Spring), Oktoberfest (Fall)

PUBLIC TRANSIT
UP-NW/Crystal Lake

12 | 180 | • | • | • | | • | • | | • | • | 3.8/5

CRYSTAL LAKE BREWING

PRO TIPS

» Dog friendly on the patio only.

» Flights come with a smart, stylish presentation: a circular wooden paddle shaped like a life preserver.

» There's often live music on Thursdays, and food trucks are known to come by on Fridays.

» A well-lit patio provides a unique, nighttime atmosphere that almost feels like it could be your neighbor's back yard.

» Tours are available Saturdays at 2p; the $10 price includes a beer and a take-home tumbler.

» Children permitted until 7p.

DATE OF VISIT:

MY RATING

☆ ☆ ☆ ☆ ☆

NOTES:

POPULAR BEERS

M	Tu	W	Th	F	S	Su
4p-10p	4p-10p	4p-10p	4p-10p	3p-12a	12p-12a	12p-9p

EMMETT'S BREWING CO.

FIELD NOTES

128 W. Main St.
West Dundee, IL
60118
847-428-4500
**emmettsbrewingco.
com**

Founder Andy Burns got his first taste of craft beer while attending Marquette University in Milwaukee. The boss at his summer job would hand him one of his home brews at the end of the shift for the two of them to share, and soon Burns was making trips to the local homebrew store himself. After a stint on the west coast in the Marines, witnessing the boom of craft beer in that hop-heavy part of the world, Burns' wish became to help pioneer a craft beer boom of his own in his native Chicagoland, naming the venture after his grandfather, Emmett in 1999.

Photo Credit: Emmett's Brewing

OWNER
Andrew Burns

HEAD BREWER
Dennis Abplanalp

AVAILABILITY
Chicago

BEST KNOWN FOR
IPAs, German ales and lagers

DATE FOUNDED
1999

2016 PRODUCTION
2,600 bbl (total)

RECENT AWARDS
GABF 2016

KEY EVENTS
Quarterly Beermaster dinners, St. Patrick's Day (Mar), New Year's Eve (Dec)

| 12 | 170 | • | • | • | • | • | • | • | 3.6/5 |

EMMETT'S BREWING CO.

PRO TIPS

» Dog friendly on the patio only.

» Emmett's has three additional locations around Chicago: Palatine (in the northwestern suburbs), Wheaton (western), and Downers Grove (southwestern).

» Each of the four locations have friendly, main street-style architecture that integrates well into Emmett's small-town, neighborhood pub ethos.

» Expect a large, family-friendly food menu that offers plenty of crowd-pleasing appetizers and small bites in various permutations, salads, sandwiches, burgers, and entrées.

» An in-house mug club will get one a special glass to drink from in-house, plus other periodic benefits.

Photo Credit: Emmett's Brewing

DATE OF VISIT:

MY RATING
☆☆☆☆☆

NOTES:

POPULAR BEERS

M	Tu	W	Th	F	S	Su
11:30-11	11:30-11	11:30-11	11:30-11	11:30-12	11:30-12	11:30-9

LIGHT THE LAMP BREWERY

FIELD NOTES

10 N. Lake St.
Grayslake, IL 60030
847-752-8489
**lightthelampbrew-
ery.com**

The people behind every brewery come together for a wide variety of reasons. This uniqueness holds true for the hockey dads of Grayslake. They always wanted a place to huddle warmly together and watch hockey, all while drinking some amazing beer. The reality of this brainchild saw its fruition in 2012 with Light The Lamp Brewery. Dan Ray, their head brewer, puts together a wide variety of styles that appeal to hockey fans and all others. And they must be on to something as they have plans to expand into larger space soon.

OWNER
Bill Hermes, Jeff Sheppard, Dave Cavanaugh

HEAD BREWER
Dan Ray

AVAILABILITY
Taproom only

BEST KNOWN FOR
Variety

DATE FOUNDED
2012

2016 PRODUCTION
217 bbl

KEY EVENTS
Host a Pond Hockey Tournament on Grayslake (Jan)

10 | 50 | • | • | • | • | • | | | • | | 3.8/5

LIGHT THE LAMP BREWERY

PRO TIPS

» Like trivia and hockey? Head over on Thursdays and you won't be disappointed.

» Keeping with their theme, all of the Light the Lamp beer names are related to hockey.

» Great meetup space after checking out the fantastic Grayslake farmers market during summer weekends.

» Stay tuned for when these guys move just across the parking lot to a new space that will include a full menu and outdoor seats (expected in late 2017).

» The new space will provide increased production capacity and the distribution of can and bottles.

» Expect to see several regular dogs and Blackhawks games on the TV.

POPULAR BEERS

Short-handed IPA	Sin Bin Stout	Red Line Ale	1980 Miracle Pale Ale

DATE OF VISIT:

MY RATING
☆ ☆ ☆ ☆ ☆

NOTES:

M	Tu	W	Th	F	S	Su
5p-10p	5p-10p	5p-10p	5p-10p	4p-12a	12p-12a	12p-6p

THE LUCKY MONK

FIELD NOTES

105 Hollywood Blvd.
South Barrington, IL
60010
847-898-0500
theluckymonk.com

South Barrington may be a ways from the city proper, but that doesn't mean its denizens don't deserve a brewpub that combines the comfort food of a local bar with house-made brews and large patio area with requisite fire pit. Lucky Monk generally offers five perennial beers and one seasonal offering for customers, in addition to six or so guest taps. Named after Belgian Trappist monks, these guys take both their beer and food very seriously, some may say to the religious experience level.

OWNER
Samatas family

HEAD BREWER
Anthony Carolio

AVAILABILITY
Brewpub only

BEST KNOWN FOR
German styles, IPAs, stouts

DATE FOUNDED
2009

2016 PRODUCTION
750 bbl

| 12 | 400 | • | | | • | | | • | • | | 3.7/5 |

THE LUCKY MONK

PRO TIPS

» Check out the Monk Society, a frequent-customer program that lets customers earn points with each purchase, and redeem points for rewards. The Society also offers discounts on growlers, bombers, and kegs to-go, plus a complimentary birthday burger, a mug, and priority seating.

» Suburban comfort and friendliness exude from the exterior before you even enter from the huge parking lot. Edison bulbs and wooden ceiling beams allow for a bit of style to triumph over suburban homogeneity.

» Try the sticky donuts for dessert.

» They have happy hour Mon-Thurs 3-6p featuring $3.50 pints and food specials.

POPULAR BEERS

Confes-sional IPA	Fallen Angel	Trittica Wheat Ale	Solitude Oatmeal Stout

DATE OF VISIT:

MY RATING
☆ ☆ ☆ ☆ ☆

NOTES:

M	Tu	W	Th	F	S	Su
11a-11p	11a-11p	11a-11p	11a-11p	11a-1a	11a-1a	11a-11p

MIKERPHONE BREWING

FIELD NOTES

Mikerphone, currently one of the Chicagoland area's buzziest breweries, is helmed by Mike Pallen. Pallen is a music industry veteran, doing everything from promoting and managing bands, to helping run the international marketing for School of Rock. Mike was previously the head brewer at the now defunct BreakRoom Brewery and SlapShot Brewing Company, along with stints at Pipeworks and 18th Street. His current venture has led him to produce several highly lauded and in-demand beers that generate plenty of excitement with each release.

121 Garlisch Dr.
Elk Grove Village, IL 60007
847-264-8904
mikerphonebrew-ing.com

OWNER
Mike Pallen, Lisa Pallen

HEAD BREWER
Mike Pallen

AVAILABILITY
Chicago - very limited

BEST KNOWN FOR
NE IPAs, sours, stouts

DATE FOUNDED
2015

2016 PRODUCTION
N/A

KEY EVENTS
Pale Pauper Day (May)

8 | 45 | | | • | • | | | | 4.4/5

MIKERPHONE BREWING

PRO TIPS

» Bottles currently see extremely limited distribution, so if you want this nectar, make sure you're willing to brave a line at the taproom (especially on the weekends) or find a store off the beaten path.

» Located in a friendly industrial park, the taproom itself is around 1,000 square feet and features plenty of guitars and amps lining the walls. The space is bright and kid-friendly.

» Bottle releases generally lead to the biggest crowds at Mikerphone, so prepare yourself if you're going during a release.

» The bottles-to-go line forms at the left door, while the taproom line forms at the right door (where you can purchase bottles-to-go as well)

POPULAR BEERS

DATE OF VISIT:

MY RATING
☆ ☆ ☆ ☆ ☆

NOTES:

M	Tu	W	Th	F	S	Su
closed	closed	closed	3p-10p	3p-10p	11a-10p	11a-7p

SCORCHED EARTH BREWING COMPANY

FIELD NOTES

Mike Dallas, with the loving kindness, and support of his wife (and brewery co-owner) Jen, started up Scorched Earth in their home in McHenry County after Mike completed past employment lives in the Air Force and public administration. Scorched Earth sports a 15-barrel system in the northwestern suburb of Algonquin. The beers themselves run the gamut from American to Belgian, hoppy to mild, dark to light, and everywhere in between.

203 Berg St.
Algonquin, IL 60102
224-209-8472
**scorchedearthbrew-
ing.com**

OWNER
Mike Dallas, Jennifer Dallas

HEAD BREWER
Mark Gres

AVAILABILITY
Chicago, IA

BEST KNOWN FOR
Cream ale, Belgians, stouts, porters

DATE FOUNDED
2014

2016 PRODUCTION
1,000 bbl

RECENT AWARDS
FoBAB 2016

KEY EVENTS
Scorched Earth Day (Jun)

| 12 | 50 | • | | • | | • | | | | | | • | | | 4.0/5 |

SCORCHED EARTH BREWING COMPANY

PRO TIPS

» Dog friendly on the patio only.

» The sizable space has a long bar with plenty of seating, as well as picnic or beer hall-style tables that offer a view of the brewery setup.

» While there's no kitchen, there are plenty of good restaurants close-by for ordering food in.

» Get in line for the shuffleboard table if you feel like you can hustle your friends.

» Trivia nights are on Thursdays at the taproom, with food trucks occasionally coming by on Fridays.

» Live music periodically at the tap room, but check ahead to see if there's a show.

DATE OF VISIT:

MY RATING
☆ ☆ ☆ ☆ ☆

NOTES:

POPULAR BEERS

M	Tu	W	Th	F	S	Su
closed	closed	closed	3p-10p	3p-10p	12p-10p	12p-7p

SIDE LOT BREWERY

FIELD NOTES

Up in Wauconda, IL, Side Lot provides its guests with a small stable of four perennial brews, a good selection of seasonal options, and a special release every now and then to make the geeks happy. Next to a gas station in a literal side lot, the space offers some well-curated guest drafts and European-inspired sandwiches. A variety of small plates complement their house brews nicely. And if you're not feeling like a beer, grab one of the ciders available instead.

110 Slocum Lake Rd.
Wauconda, IL
60084
847-865-0281
sidelotbrewing.com

OWNER
Phil Castello,
Brittany Barth,
Jason Vucic

HEAD BREWER
Phil Castello

AVAILABILITY
Brewpub only

BEST KNOWN FOR
IPAs, range of
European styles

DATE FOUNDED
2015

2016 PRODUCTION
120 bbl

| 16 | 60 | • | • | • | • | | • | • | 3.7/5 |

SIDE LOT BREWERY

PRO TIPS

» Dog friendly on the patio only (which is huge at 85 seats).

» The entrance is off the side lot near the Citgo station in Wauconda, but the space itself is leisurely and inviting, with couches, TVs, and bar seating aplenty.

» Beer and yoga is hosted every month or so, and the cost covers some beer after the class is done.

» The food menu is carefully put together with some surprisingly fancy offerings. Candied bacon and a bacon jam small plate both make the carnivore's mouth water, while whipped feta with pepper jelly and fresh bread is downright decadent.

DATE OF VISIT:

MY RATING
☆ ☆ ☆ ☆ ☆

NOTES:

POPULAR BEERS

Jimmy The Weasel	Cocky Wood-pecker IPA	Cocky Wood-pecker IPA	Smokin' Squirrel

M	Tu	W	Th	F	S	Su
closed	11a-11p	11a-11p	11a-11p	11a-12a	11a-12a	11a-8p

TIGHTHEAD BREWING COMPANY

FIELD NOTES

Tighthead's tagline is "worth more than a try" and for this north-suburban brewery, they've proven themselves more than up to the task. Owner and head brewer Bruce Dir got the itch for brewing in 1993, when his then-fiancée/now-wife gave him a homebrew kit for Christmas. Eighteen years and an education at the Siebel Institute of Technology later, Tighthead Brewing opened in Mundelein in 2011. The name "Tighthead" is a rugby position term, thus explaining the flaming rugby ball in the brewery's logo.

161 N. Archer Ave.
Mundelein, IL 60060
847-970-9174
**tightheadbrewing.
com**

OWNER
Bruce Dir

HEAD BREWER
Bruce Dir, Billy Oaks

AVAILABILITY
IL, WI

BEST KNOWN FOR
IPAs, pales, reds, Belgians

DATE FOUNDED
2011

2016 PRODUCTION
2,525 bbl

KEY EVENTS
Mundelein Beer Fest (Jun), Hoptoberfest (Sept)

PUBLIC TRANSIT
NCS/Mundelein

16 | 140 | • | • | • | • | • | • | • | 4.0/5

TIGHTHEAD BREWING COMPANY

PRO TIPS

» "Pints and Poses" is Tighthead's monthly yoga series on each first Sunday. $20 will get you an hour of yoga and 2 pints at the taproom.

» The brewery's merchandise store features prints of can label art, hand-crafted beer soap, label-themed Swiss Army knives, and even logo-emblazoned rugby balls for the aspiring rugger in the family.

» Major supporter of the Mundelein Craft Beer Festival, which celebrated its 6th iteration in June 2017.

» Board games are available. On Wednesdays they have trivia and live music Thursdays and occasionally on the weekends.

DATE OF VISIT:

MY RATING
☆ ☆ ☆ ☆ ☆

NOTES:

POPULAR BEERS

M	Tu	W	Th	F	S	Su
4p-10p	4p-10p	4p-10p	4p-10p	12p-11p	12p-11p	12p-6p

VILLAGE VINTNER WINERY & BREWERY

FIELD NOTES

Doesn't a vintner make wine? Yes. So, what is Village Vintner, a winery that's been around since 2005 doing in a taproom guide? Well, they decided just crafting wine wasn't enough and opened up a brewery in 2012, making them the only such combination business in the entire area. Housed in a huge space in Algonquin, this combination facility also sports a wood-fired oven for pizzas and other entrées.

2380 Esplanade Dr.
Algonquin, IL 60102
847-658-4900
**thevillagevintner.
com**

OWNER
Steve Boyer, Bob Boyer

HEAD BREWER
Steve Boyer, Brett Boyer

AVAILABILITY
Brewpub only

BEST KNOWN FOR
IPAs, cream ales, British styles

DATE FOUNDED
2012

2016 PRODUCTION
300 bbl

| 12 | 125 | • | | • | • | | • | • | | 3.5/5 |

VILLAGE VINTNER WINERY & BREWERY

PRO TIPS

» The space is a multi-level suburban brick building that features plenty of bar seating and tables.

» The food menu makes use of the wood-fired oven, sure, but check out the mozzarella-prosciutto roll; they're made daily.

» A more adventurous person might suggest opting for the cashew and pear pizza or pesto and asparagus instead of a standard red pie, or you have the choice of designing your own pizza, too.

» The wine and growler club is free to join, and offers a discount on the monthly purchase of bottles or a growler, plus a tasting of beers or wines.

DATE OF VISIT:

MY RATING

NOTES:

POPULAR BEERS

Hoprock-et IPA	Coconilla Stout	Vanilla Cream Ale	Bourbon Barrel Aged Ale

M	Tu	W	Th	F	S	Su
5p-10p	11a-10p	11a-10p	11a-10p	11-11:30	11-11:30	12p-9p

WILD ONION BREWERY

FIELD NOTES

22221 N. Pepper Rd.
Lake Barrington, IL
60010
847-381-7308
onionbrewery.com

Wild Onion Brewery began in 1996 as a production-only operation, but the idea of opening a brewpub always lingered in minds of the Kainz family. A lottery jackpot win in 2000 led to the opening of the pub in 2003. The original 1996 brewery was constructed out of old dairy equipment in a warehouse. Today, the production brewery sits below the pub itself among a 20-acre complex (a former gravel quarry) that houses the Onion Brewery's green initiative. The restoration turned what had been an impromptu dump into a beautiful nature site.

OWNER
Mike Kainz, John Kainz

HEAD BREWER
Peter Janusas

AVAILABILITY
IL, MO, NJ

BEST KNOWN FOR
IPAs, stouts

DATE FOUNDED
1996

2016 PRODUCTION
3,100 bbl

RECENT AWARDS
FoBAB 2016

18 | 135 | • | • | • | • | • | • | 3.6/5

WILD ONION BREWERY

PRO TIPS

» The woodwork inside this lodge-like complex of brewpub and banquet hall is simply stunning. Featuring some rescued timbers from the Revolutionary War era, the Onion pub features a large, intricately cut, multi-sided bar that has plenty of seating, as well large comfortable booths and tables, and even a stone fireplace in the middle of the pub.

» The menu has just enough variations on the pub grub theme to keep it interesting.

» The pub's Great Hall is a huge reception space used mainly for weddings. When it's booked (most weekends in the summer), the outdoor space is closed. So call ahead if you hope to sit on the beautiful patio.

DATE OF VISIT:

MY RATING
☆ ☆ ☆ ☆ ☆

NOTES:

POPULAR BEERS

M	Tu	W	Th	F	S	Su
closed	11a-11p	11a-11p	11a-11p	11a-12a	11a-12a	11a-8p

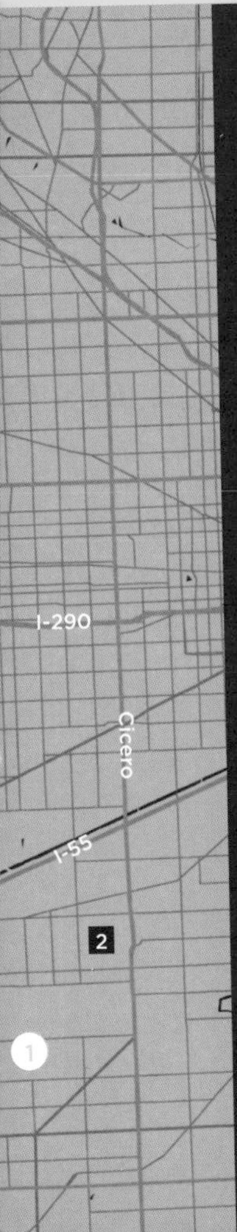

SUBURBS WEST

1. 5 Rabbit Cerveceria
2. Alter Brewing Company
3. Blue Nose Brewery
4. BuckleDown Brewing
5. Church Street Brewing Company
6. Exit Strategy Brewing Co.
7. Flapjack Brewery
8. Imperial Oak Brewing
9. Itasca Brewing Company
10. Kinslahger Brewing Company
11. Lunar Brewing Co.
12. Miskatonic Brewing Company
13. Myths and Legends Brewing Company
14. Noon Whistle Brewing
15. Oak Park Brewing Company
16. Skeleton Key Brewery

I-290

Cicero

I-55

2

NEIGHBORHOOD HIGHLIGHTS

1 O'Hare Int'l Airport
2 Midway Int'l Airport
3 Toyota Park
4 Frank Lloyd Wright Home & Studio
5 Brookfield Zoo

5 RABBIT CERVECERIA

FIELD NOTES

6398 W. 74th St.
Bedford Park, IL
60638
312-895-9591
5rabbitbrewery.com

5 Rabbit is the United States' first Latin American-inspired brewery. The brewery's creative director, Randy Mosher, is one of Chicago's legends of craft beer and author of one of the definitive craft beer tomes, Tasting Beer. 5 Rabbit's beers take inspiration from Latin American culture and cuisine for their unique flavors and style choices. In June 2016, 5 Rabbit gained national press for their blonde ale, Chinga tu Pelo, a not-at-all subtle jibe at a certain presidential candidate's infamous coiffure.

OWNER
Andres Araya,
Randy Mosher

HEAD BREWER
Nathan Chesser

AVAILABILITY
Chicago, FL, IN, OH

BEST KNOWN FOR
Fruit beers, lighter styles

DATE FOUNDED
2011

2016 PRODUCTION
8,000 bbl

RECENT AWARDS
FoBAB 2016

8 | 80 | • | • | • | • | | | • | | 3.8/5

5 RABBIT CERVECERIA

PRO TIPS

» Cleverly nicknamed "The Rabbit Hole," 5 Rabbit's Bedford Park facility is less than two miles from Toyota Park, home of MLS' Chicago Fire, so combining both experiences into one day would make for an ideal suburban excursion.

» Latin American inspired artwork adorns the space, which features several tables, but no bar seating.

» Movies on the wall and a foosball table are available for entertainment.

» Look for beers with culinary flair, featuring spices and foods from Latin America.

» Food trucks will occasionally show up, but the taproom is BYOF, too.

» Each week they release a taproom only beer.

DATE OF VISIT:

MY RATING
☆ ☆ ☆ ☆ ☆

NOTES:

POPULAR BEERS

M	Tu	W	Th	F	S	Su
closed	closed	4p-10p	4p-10p	4p-11p	1p-9p	closed

ALTER BREWING COMPANY

FIELD NOTES

2300 Wisconsin Ave.
Downers Grove, IL
60515
630-541-9558
alterbrewing.com

Alter opened in 2013, bringing craft beer to the western suburb of Downers Grove. The taproom features 12 drafts that run the gamut of styles, taste profiles, and alcohol strengths with an impressive level of economy. Hopheads and dark beer fans will be pleased alongside sour aficionados and drinkers of session beers. The space itself features a high ceiling, plenty of seating at the bar, a "roomy-industrial space" that gets accents from orange chairs and plenty of wood accents, especially behind the bar. For a suburban taproom, this looks and feels pretty hip.

OWNER
Mark Hedrick,
David Yob, Pete
Kosanovich

HEAD BREWER
Mark Hedrick

AVAILABILITY
Chicago - limited
draft only

BEST KNOWN FOR
IPAs, blonde ales

DATE FOUNDED
2015

2016 PRODUCTION
755 bbl

RECENT AWARDS
FoBAB 2016

KEY EVENTS
AlterFest (Oct),
Anniversary Party
(Dec)

PUBLIC TRANSIT
BNSF/Belmont

| 12 | 106 | | | • | • | • | | • | • | 4.0/5 |

ALTER BREWING COMPANY

PRO TIPS

» Alter features trivia every Tuesday night. Yoga sessions also take place periodically on Saturdays, with an hour of yoga and a beer offered for a combined $15.

» No food menu, but food trucks do come occasionally.

» It should be noted that, like some other suburban breweries, Alter has a 48 ounce per person limit on beer that can be served on site, so, as their menu says, choose wisely.

» If you're looking to join the growler club, your $350 sign up fee will get you one growler fill per week, invitations to the club's yearly BBQ and the brewery's yearly festival, plus a fancy, double-walled, vacuum-insulated growler.

POPULAR BEERS

ALTERior Motive IPA	Dank You DIPA	Alto Porto Porter	Alto Porto Porter

M	Tu	W	Th	F	S	Su
3p-10p	3p-10p	3p-10p	3p-10p	12p-11p	12p-11p	12p-8p

DATE OF VISIT:

MY RATING

NOTES:

BLUE NOSE BREWERY

FIELD NOTES

6119 East Ave.
Hodgkins, IL 60525
708-905-5198
**bluenosebrewery.
com**

A suburban strip mall in Hodgkins, IL, is the setting for Blue Nose, formerly of the equally small town of Justice, both in the southwest suburbs. Blue Nose has been known to collaborate with other breweries, including Tim Hoerman's 51st Ward Brewing. The two collaborated on a Cubs-themed barrel-aged saison simply called "The 2016." It was brewed on Opening Day and bottled during the now-famous, losing streak-ending World Series. Blue Nose is meant to be a neighborhood gathering place that strives to be "spacious yet cozy," fitting for its suburban audience.

OWNER
Nathan Garcia,
Jordan Isenberg

HEAD BREWER
Jordan Isenberg,
Justin Rigoni

AVAILABILITY
Chicago - limited

BEST KNOWN FOR
Belgians, pales, IPAs

DATE FOUNDED
2012

2016 PRODUCTION
750 bbl

| 10 | 250 | • | • | • | • | | | • | | 4.0/5 |

BLUE NOSE BREWERY

PRO TIPS

» The taproom is a bright, friendly space with brushed-metal furniture and a bright blue floor in the brewing space.

» Chicago sports teams get plenty of screen time with sound on the big screen.

» Periodically hosts tournaments of favorite old school video games.

» The brewery's dog, also featured in the logo of the brewery, is a semi-regular visitor to the space.

» Blue Nose often partners with the Ofrenda food truck, offering a semi-traditional Taco Tuesday that's always a crowd pleaser.

» They have a pool table and cornhole set to entertain while drinking.

DATE OF VISIT:

MY RATING
☆ ☆ ☆ ☆ ☆

NOTES:

POPULAR BEERS

Archer Ave.	Saison Saran-don	XXX Honey	The Other

M	Tu	W	Th	F	S	Su
3p-12a	3p-12a	3p-12a	3p-12a	12p-2a	12p-2a	12p-10p

BUCKLEDOWN BREWING

FIELD NOTES

8700 W. 47th St.
Lyons, IL 60534
708-777-1842
**buckledownbrew-
ing.com**

Sean Mahoney and Ike Orcutt founded BuckleDown in the small southwestern suburb of Lyons, with an ethos similar to that of their surroundings: hard working, honest people looking to make the sorts of beers that they like to drink themselves. Their beers are a studied mix of hop-forward American styles and observantly made Belgian ales. Their main flagship beers are drinkable, proletarian, and hop-forward. Beyond the flagships, don't miss their collaboration beers with places like Kuma's, Greenbush and Haymarket.

OWNER
Sean Mahoney, Ike Orcutt

HEAD BREWER
Ike Orcutt

AVAILABILITY
Chicago

BEST KNOWN FOR
Pales, IPAs, seasonal lagers

DATE FOUNDED
2013

2016 PRODUCTION
2,500 bbl

KEY EVENTS
Oktoberfest (Sept)

10 | 75 | | | • | • | | | | • | | 3.8/5

BUCKLEDOWN BREWING

PRO TIPS

» Bright yellow stools at the bar are the first thing that catches the eye at the otherwise wood, metal, and concrete-adorned taproom.

» Plenty of brewpub exclusives can be had in addition to the normal roll call of flagship and perennial beers.

» Live music is a feature almost every weekend.

» There may not be outdoor seating, but the big garage door to the brewery opens to let some breeze and sunshine in.

» Their big annual release is for Barrel-Aged Shadowbox; typically a few variants of Shadowbox are on draft only at the tap room.

» Food trucks on the weekends.

DATE OF VISIT:

MY RATING
☆ ☆ ☆ ☆ ☆

NOTES:

POPULAR BEERS

M	Tu	W	Th	F	S	Su
closed	closed	4p-10p	12p-10p	12p-11p	12p-11p	12p-5p

CHURCH STREET BREWING COMPANY

FIELD NOTES

Located 10 miles west of Chicago in suburban Itasca, Church Street specializes mostly in continental European styles that don't often see production in the United States, let alone in Chicago. Sure, the Brimstone IPA is the bone they throw to those who firmly believe that an American brewery simply cannot exist without a hoppy offering, but dig deeper and you'll find some lovely examples of styles that you'd normally only find fresh across the pond.

1480 Industrial Dr.
Itasca, IL 60143
630-438-5725
**churchstreetbrew.
com**

OWNER
Lisa Gregor, Joe Gregor

HEAD BREWER
TJ Bachorz

AVAILABILITY
IL, FL, MO

BEST KNOWN FOR
Lagers, pilsners, seasonal German styles

DATE FOUNDED
2012

2016 PRODUCTION
2,300 bbl

8 | 150 | • | • | • | | | | • | | 3.9/5

CHURCH STREET BREWING COMPANY

PRO TIPS

» Cinder block walls get adorned with plenty of decorative bottles, metal tack signs, and hung frames, turning what could be a drab industrial space into an inviting, busy, and friendly taproom that proclaims "NO WORKING DURING DRINKING HOURS."

» Seating is a couple of modest folding tables, picnic tables, and some barrels with stools surrounding; it's minimal but homey.

» Food trucks will come by occasionally, but otherwise there's no kitchen.

» Ping-pong table available and live music most Saturdays for entertainment.

DATE OF VISIT:

MY RATING

☆ ☆ ☆ ☆ ☆

NOTES:

POPULAR BEERS

M	Tu	W	Th	F	S	Su
5p-10p	5p-10p	5p-10p	5p-10p	4p-11p	12p-11p	12p-7p

EXIT STRATEGY BREWING CO.

FIELD NOTES

7700 Madison St.
Forest Park, IL
60130
708-689-8771
**exitstrategybrew-
ing.com**

Don't let the plain, rustic outside deter you from checking out this brewery. A short 10 minute walk from the Forest Park blue line stop, the inside will completely blow you away. As the first and only brewery in Forest Park, owner/ brewmaster Chris Valleau and co-owner Katherine Valleau looked to create a nice blend of metropolitan living and suburban lifestyle. As a home brewer for many years winning over 40 awards across the country, their beers represent classic styles, modernized.

OWNER
Chris Valleau,
Katherine Valleau

HEAD BREWER
Chris Valleau

AVAILABILITY
Chicago - limited
draft only

BEST KNOWN FOR
IPAs, pales, fruit
beers, brown/
Scottish ales

DATE FOUNDED
2015

2016 PRODUCTION
450 bbl

KEY EVENTS
Anniversary Party
(Apr)

PUBLIC TRANSIT
'L' Blue/Forest Park

16	140	•		•			•	•		•	3.9/5

EXIT STRATEGY BREWING CO.

PRO TIPS

» Not feeling beer? They also have an entire list comprised of wine, cocktails and non-alcoholic options, including their own house made sodas.

» They offer an arrangement of food items from small plates and sandwiches to full blown meals (the burger is the best).

» Make sure to check out the overhead lamps at the bar. The bulb shades are different brewery growlers (Pintrest would approve).

» They have their mainstay beers but also have "lab beers" which are seasonal/one-offs.

» 21 and up only at the bar seats, but highchairs are available for future craft fans everywhere else.

POPULAR BEERS

Judg-mental Dick	Perse-phone	Exit Strategy Pale Ale	Valleau-dated

DATE OF VISIT:

MY RATING
☆ ☆ ☆ ☆ ☆

NOTES:

M	Tu	W	Th	F	S	Su
closed	3p-10p	3p-10p	3p-10p	3p-12a	11a-12a	11a-4p

FLAPJACK BREWERY

FIELD NOTES

6833 Stanley Ave.
Berwyn, IL 60402
708-637-4030
**flapjackbrewery.
com**

The "Established 2013" in the Flapjack logo is a reminder of how challenging it can be to open a brewery. It may have taken longer than expected for brothers Paul and James Macchione after they launched a Kickstarter campaign in 2014, but they finally opened their brewpub in May 2017 in Berwyn's Historic Depot District. The small batch brewery space features an open kitchen with a wood fired oven for a selection of neapolitan pizzas (prepared by James) to pair with your beers.

OWNER
Paul Macchione,
James Macchione

HEAD BREWER
Paul Macchione

AVAILABILITY
Brewpub only

BEST KNOWN FOR
Lighter ales

DATE FOUNDED
2013

2016 PRODUCTION
N/A

PUBLIC TRANSIT
BNSF/Berwyn

8 | 60 | | | • | | • | | • | NA/5

FLAPJACK BREWERY

PRO TIPS

» The welcoming and friendly brewpub just opened at press time so we expect the somewhat bare space to add a bit more character in the months ahead.

» Flapjack was the owner Paul's nickname in high school due to his love of pancakes.

» Short walk from the Metra Berwyn stop. If driving, can pair with visits to Kinslahger, Oak Park Brewing and Exit Strategy.

» The family connection continues at Flapjack as brother-in-law Joey is the assistant brewer and a bartender.

DATE OF VISIT:

MY RATING
☆ ☆ ☆ ☆ ☆

NOTES:

POPULAR BEERS

Fantasmo Vanilla Cream

Boltneck Coffee Stout

M	Tu	W	Th	F	S	Su
closed	closed	2p-10p	2p-10p	2p-10p	12p-10p	closed

IMPERIAL OAK BREWING

FIELD NOTES

IMPERIAL OAK
BREWING
ESTD 2013

501 Willow Blvd.
Willow Springs, IL
60480
708-330-5096
**imperialoakbrewing.
com**

Right off the Des Plaines (pronounced DEZZ PLAYNZ by the true Chicagoan) River, and minimal distance from several woods and nature preserves, Imperial Oak opened in 2014 with a small, 7-barrel system that allows for the production and release of plenty of new beers on a near-constant basis. The constant churn-and-burn of new beers coming on and off means that even regulars are treated to new options to taste with each visit. Options will range from the lighter, more universal crowd-pleasers to the heavy hitters for the initiated and voracious.

Photo Credit: Grant Hamilton

OWNER
Grant Hamilton,
Chris DiBraccio,
Brett Semenske

HEAD BREWER
Brett Semenske

AVAILABILITY
Taproom only

BEST KNOWN FOR
IPAs, stouts,
Belgians

DATE FOUNDED
2014

2016 PRODUCTION
890 bbl

KEY EVENTS
Anniversary
Party (Jun), St.
Patrick's Day (Mar),
Oktoberfest (Sept)

PUBLIC TRANSIT
HC/Willow Springs

20 | 175 | • | • | • | • | • | | | | • | 4.2/5

IMPERIAL OAK BREWING

PRO TIPS

» Dog friendly on the patio only.

» No kitchen, but offers a full bar, replete with cider, liquor, wine, and cyser options.

» There's some table seating inside, but if the weather's nice, there's no reason for you to not be out on their large sunny patio.

» Plenty of food trucks come by on Friday, Saturday, and Sunday, but it's always best to check in advance.

» For the nature and cycling lover, the location is a dream, adjacent to the Des Plaines River and the Illinois Centennial Trail. If you have a day to kill, and a decent bike, this is an ideal way to spend your time.

Photo Credit: Terry Hamilton

DATE OF VISIT:

MY RATING
☆ ☆ ☆ ☆ ☆

NOTES:

POPULAR BEERS

Predic-tion... Pain?	Crank It Hop	Udderly Black	Crank It Dank

M	Tu	W	Th	F	S	Su
3p-11p	3p-11p	12p-11p	12p-1a	12p-1a	12p-1a	11a-10p

ITASCA BREWING COMPANY

FIELD NOTES

While they've been brewing since 2011, early in 2017 Itasca Brewing decided to call Itasca Country Club their home. Open to the public, guests are not required to have a membership in order to enjoy some refreshing beers (sorry, no golf is included). Despite the small space, there are still quite a few options for every beer lover's enjoyment, including an adjacent restaurant for hungry drinkers. With the fermentation tanks directly behind the bar, no need for a brewery tour - you're sitting in it.

400 E. Orchard St.
Itasca, IL 60143
630-773-1800
itascabrewingcompany.com

OWNER
Not provided

HEAD BREWER
Michael Valente

AVAILABILITY
Taproom only

BEST KNOWN FOR
English styles, pales

DATE FOUNDED
2011

2016 PRODUCTION
300 bbl

| 14 | 100 | | | • | • | | | • | | 4.0/5 |

ITASCA BREWING COMPANY

PRO TIPS

» Take note of the unusual open times/ days before making the trip - only a few hours on Friday, Saturday and Sunday.

» Make sure to call in advance. They do close often for private events. After all, it's a country club.

» A restaurant, Fox and Turtle, is located behind the taproom in case you are hungry - order directly while seated in the taproom.

» It is a country club, so sloppy attire could be an issue. Keep your favorite cut-off drinking shorts at home.

DATE OF VISIT:

MY RATING
☆ ☆ ☆ ☆ ☆

NOTES:

POPULAR BEERS

Citra Session Pale Ale   Bean Smith

M	Tu	W	Th	F	S	Su
closed	closed	closed	closed	6p-9p	6p-9p	12p-4p

KINSLAHGER BREWING COMPANY

FIELD NOTES

6806 Roosevelt Rd.
Oak Park, IL 60304
844-552-4437
kinslahger.com

Forget the road rage of driving and hop on the CTA blue line to get to this darling new brewery. Just half a mile from the Oak Park El stop, the taproom looks like another commercial space, until you step inside. The taproom is decorated with black and white photos and a classic bar feel; its easy to see why this is a local must-stop. Kinslahger is a mash up of three things: Kinship (connection of individuals), lager (their focus beer) and the three owner's first letter of their last names. Despite the small and narrow space, it maximizes the area in order to create cozy comfort.

OWNER
Steve Loranz, Neal Armstrong, Keith Huizinga

HEAD BREWER
Steve Loranz

AVAILABILITY
Chicago - limited

BEST KNOWN FOR
Lagers

DATE FOUNDED
2016

2016 PRODUCTION
N/A

PUBLIC TRANSIT
'L' Blue/Oak Park

12 | 48 | | | • | • | | | | • | 4.3/5

KINSLAHGER BREWING COMPANY

PRO TIPS

» In addition to offering a few snacks (start with an appetizer of the combo plate or cheese, pretzel and sausage for $10), they are bring your own food and regularly host food trucks.

» Small space so be prepared if bringing larger groups. Can get quickly crowded on the weekend.

» While they tell you not to tip (multiple times), all tips get donated to the American Federation for Suicide Prevention! So still tip.

» No cash, so bring your plastic or Apple pay.

» There are a couple of music venues nearby (Fitzgerald's and Wire) - so get your pre-show drink here.

DATE OF VISIT:

MY RATING
☆ ☆ ☆ ☆ ☆

NOTES:

POPULAR BEERS

Chicago Common	Dunkel	Baltic Poter	Prohibition Pilsner

M	Tu	W	Th	F	S	Su
closed	closed	3p-10p	3p-10p	3p-10p	11a-10p	12p-5p

LUNAR BREWING CO.

FIELD NOTES

Lunar is old-school. Some may call it a dive. Outside appearances might put off some potential newcomers. It's got wood-paneling, a darker sort of ambiance lit primarily by neon signs, and an overall outside impression that, if you're driving by, you could blink and you'll probably miss it. However, if you're looking for craft beer and a place that takes you to the look and feel of a Chicago bar from back in your grandparents' day, this long-running establishment is the place.

54 E. St. Charles Rd.
Villa Park, IL 60181
630-530-2077

OWNER
Charlie Tierney

HEAD BREWER
Jonathan Eichholz

AVAILABILITY
Taproom only

BEST KNOWN FOR
Variety

DATE FOUNDED
1996

2016 PRODUCTION
115 bbl

PUBLIC TRANSIT
UP-W/Villa Park

17 | 105 | . | . | . | . | | . | . | 3.9/5

LUNAR BREWING CO.

PRO TIPS

» More of a "local watering hole" than a "brewpub," and for that reason it should be loved and treasured.

» Beers are made on a very small scale. Real small. They're brewed in soup kettles. So, every batch is rare and exclusive.

» The owner has been known to sit at the bar and socialize with guests, so feel free to introduce yourself.

» No website (really old school), so don't try to get their latest draft list online.

» Very friendly regulars - be sure to strike up a conversation.

DATE OF VISIT:

MY RATING

NOTES:

POPULAR BEERS

| Moon-dance IPA | Raspber-ry Cream | Total Eclipse Stout | Neil Arm-strong |

M	Tu	W	Th	F	S	Su
12p-1a	12p-1a	12p-1a	12p-1a	12p-2a	12p-2a	12p-1a

MISKATONIC BREWING COMPANY

FIELD NOTES

1000 N. Frontage Rd.
Darien, IL 60561
630-541-9414
**miskatonicbrewing.
com**

If the works of horror fiction writer H.P. Lovecraft inspired you to start a brewery, these folks beat you to it (Miskatonic was the name of a fictional university in Lovecraftian lore). Miskatonic is the collective creation of a couple alums from Chicago area's best-known breweries. Brewery manager and co-founder Josh Mowry arrives from Two Brothers, while head brewer John Wyskiewicz used to ply his trade at Gordon Biersch and Goose Island. Together, they craft unique brews that recreate classic and well-loved styles.

OWNER
Josh Mowry, John
Wyzkiewicz

HEAD BREWER
John Wyzkiewicz

AVAILABILITY
Chicago

BEST KNOWN FOR
IPAs, pales, English
styles, saisons

DATE FOUNDED
2015

2016 PRODUCTION
792 bbl

KEY EVENTS
Anniversary Party
(Jul)

| 10 | 115 | • | • | • | • | | • | | | • | | 3.9/5 |

MISKATONIC BREWING COMPANY

PRO TIPS

- » Bright, cinder block tasting room with a copper-clad bar.
- » Occasionally features food trucks, or just bring your own food.
- » Plenty of board game options are available in the taproom for those inclined.
- » Trivia night happens on a fairly regular basis, usually on Wednesdays.
- » Credit card only; they don't accept cash.
- » Fun fact: taproom manager AJ Blume is also an award-winning affineur (someone that ages cheeses until they're ready to eat).

DATE OF VISIT:

MY RATING

☆ ☆ ☆ ☆ ☆

NOTES:

POPULAR BEERS

M	Tu	W	Th	F	S	Su
closed	3p-10p	3p-10p	3p-10p	3p-11p	12p-11p	12p-7p

MYTHS AND LEGENDS BREWING CO.

FIELD NOTES

1115 Zygmunt Cir.
Westmont, IL 60559
630-442-7864
**mythsandlegends-
beer.com**

Myths and Legends Brewing began in 2013 as Urban Legend, with the concept that all of their beers would be named after famed legends and tales of the recent (and sometimes, distant) past. The brewery changed its name to Myths and Legends in 2016, but has continued to stick with its tried-and-true M.O. of producing a well-tuned mix of sessionable brews and bigger, imperial beers for the more enthusiastic drinker.

OWNER
Jason Hancock,
Andrew Matt, Tom
Budreck, Bob
Behrens, Shannon
Hancock

HEAD BREWER
David Leeds

AVAILABILITY
Chicago

BEST KNOWN FOR
Pales, imperial ales

DATE FOUNDED
2013

2016 PRODUCTION
N/A

KEY EVENTS
Summer Party (Jun),
Legends of the Fall
(Sept), Day of the
Dead (Oct)

10 | 40 | | | • | | • | • | | | • | | 4.0/5

MYTHS AND LEGENDS BREWING CO.

PRO TIPS

» Occupies a space in an otherwise nondescript modern-yet-industrial looking building that could be mistaken anywhere else for an anonymous warehouse.

» Though there isn't much seating at the bar, there are plenty of tables to sit at, barrels to stand around, and even a couple of couches in the corner for those feeling a bit more sedentary.

» Has a "Legends Club," which, for a small fee, allows members first crack at reserving barrel-aged and other special release bottles, a pass to their annual summer and taproom anniversary parties, a logo'd pint glass, and a small discount in the merchandise shop.

» Live music on Wednesdays.

POPULAR BEERS

The Creature	Cooper's Parachute	Catherine The Great	Scylla's Grasp

DATE OF VISIT:

MY RATING
☆ ☆ ☆ ☆ ☆

NOTES:

M	Tu	W	Th	F	S	Su
closed	5p-10p	5p-10p	5p-10p	3p-12a	12p-12a	12p-8p

NOON WHISTLE BREWING

FIELD NOTES

800 E. Roosevelt Rd.
Lombard, IL 60148
630-376-6895
noonwhistlebrew-ing.com

Usually it takes an extreme amount of hops or alcohol for a brewery to gain some buzz around craft beer circles. Noon Whistle is slowly but surely flipping that script, with a remarkably consistent stream of sessionable brews that always seem to impress. Going strong since 2014, Noon Whistle's main offerings all range between 4-6% ABV, and they're able to pack a bunch of flavor into these brews. Their "Smack" series of sours are great for enthusiasts of tart beers, but are approachable enough for novices to craft beer to expand their horizons.

OWNER
Paul Kreiner, Mike Condon, Jim Cagle

HEAD BREWER
Paul Kreiner

AVAILABILITY
Chicago

BEST KNOWN FOR
Session ales, sours, NE IPAs

DATE FOUNDED
2014

2016 PRODUCTION
1,100 bbl

| 10 | 80 | • | • | • | • | | | • | | 3.9/5 |

NOON WHISTLE BREWING

PRO TIPS

» You can still find imperial-strength beers at Noon Whistle including, a maple-syrup Barleywine, and an imperial version of their Bernie Milk Stout.

» There's no kitchen, but you can bring your own food. Food trucks are featured on Fridays.

» Their parking lot is shared with an adjacent Whirlyball (a game that mixes jai alai, basketball, and bumper cars), though we cannot recommend filling up on a bunch of session ales and then piloting a bumper car around.

» Full size drafts are $4 all day on Tuesday and Wednesday, with growler deals on Thursday.

DATE OF VISIT:

MY RATING
☆ ☆ ☆ ☆ ☆

NOTES:

POPULAR BEERS

| Cozmo | Bernie | Face Smack | Guava Gose Smack |

M	Tu	W	Th	F	S	Su
closed	12p-10p	12p-10p	12p-10p	12p-11p	12p-11p	12p-7p

OAK PARK BREWING COMPANY

FIELD NOTES

Oak Park was another longtime-dry suburb of Chicago (see also: Wheaton & Evanston), opening itself back up to alcohol sales in 1972. But, it took another 40+ years for its first brewery to open. Oak Park is a sister project of the Hamburger Mary's team, so expect a couple of shared beer recipes, more clever beer names, and the same sports bar with a ton of camp-atmosphere that you'll find at the Andersonville mainstay. As a friendly, neighborhood brewpub that just might happen to have a drag show going on next door, this unique business is filling a need in Oak Park.

155 S. Oak Park Ave.
Oak Park, IL 60302
708-445-0272
oakparkbeer.com

OWNER
Brandon Wright,
Ashley Wright, Jim
Cozzins

HEAD BREWER
Jim Cozzins

AVAILABILITY
Brewpub only

BEST KNOWN FOR
Pales, Belgians,
lagers

DATE FOUNDED
2016

2016 PRODUCTION
320 bbl

PUBLIC TRANSIT
'L' Green/Oak Park

| 16 | 100 | • | | • | • | | • | | • | 3.3/5 |

OAK PARK BREWING COMPANY

PRO TIPS

» Much like Hamburger Mary's, there's seating at the bar, with plenty of tables, booths, nooks, and hodgepodge decorations.

» The entrance has a British-style police call box familiar to fans of the TV series Doctor Who.

» The pub grub available here is a bit different from Hamburger Mary's, with spent grain flatbreads and veggie burgers featuring the brewery's used husks.

» HamBINGO Mary's is every Tuesday night, trivia night is every Wednesday, and comedy night is every Thursday. Friday and Saturday evenings feature Dining with the Divas, a dinner-and-drag show, Mary-oke (karaoke).

POPULAR BEERS

Frank Lloyd Rye IPA	Speak-easy Saison

M	Tu	W	Th	F	S	Su
11:30-10	11:30-10	11:30-10	11:30-10	11:30-12	11:30-12	11:30-10

DATE OF VISIT:

MY RATING

NOTES:

SKELETON KEY BREWERY

FIELD NOTES

WOODRIDGE, IL

8102 Lemont Rd.
Woodridge, IL 60517
630-395-9033
**skeletonkeybrewery.
com**

Skeleton Key aims to be a neighborhood community hub, and an incubator of sorts for potential brewers. They offer a program called "Spare Keys," which, for the ambitious but hesitant homebrewer looking to start their own new brewery project, is a 12-week immersion program going through all the nitty gritty in running a production brewery. Consideration for the program is done through Skeleton Key's homebrew contest, the finalists of which may qualify for the Spare Keys program. They even offer to contract brew the winning beer for the program participant.

OWNER
Emily Slayton, Paul
Slayton, John Szopa

HEAD BREWER
John Szopa

AVAILABILITY
Chicago - very
limited

BEST KNOWN FOR
Pales, IPAs, dark
ales, witbiers

DATE FOUNDED
2016

2016 PRODUCTION
80 bbl

KEY EVENTS
Anniversary Party/
Halloween Bash
(Oct)

8 | 100 | | | • | | • | | • | | 4.0/5

SKELETON KEY BREWERY

PRO TIPS

» Skeleton Key's not just here to sell beer, they want to educate, too. Book a beer education class in advance (they sell out quickly) to learn about topics like Belgian styles and becoming a beer judge.

» Two separate bar-like seating areas can accommodate as many as 20, with tables and barrels for the rest of the crowd.

» Look for food trucks on the weekends.

» One tap at the taproom is reserved for experimental beers that are only available to members of Skeleton Key's Skullmuggery Society. Members get to drink out of skull-shaped glassware and drink the special beer. Reservations to that exclusive group become available every month.

Photo Credit: DWL Images

DATE OF VISIT:

MY RATING
☆ ☆ ☆ ☆ ☆

NOTES:

POPULAR BEERS

| Friends Don't Lie | Saudade | Kings And Streetsweepers | Space Plans |

M	Tu	W	Th	F	S	Su
closed	closed	4p-10p	4p-10p	3p-11p	12p-11p	12p-6p

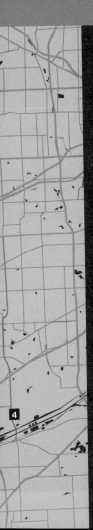

SUBURBS FAR WEST

1. BBGB Brewery & Hop Farm
2. Dry City Brew Works
3. Hopvine Brewing Co.
4. Metal Monkey Brewing
5. Nevin's Brewing Company
6. Penrose Brewing Company
7. Solemn Oath Brewery
8. Two Brothers Artisan Brewing
9. Werk Force Brewing Co.

NEIGHBORHOOD HIGHLIGHTS

1 Fermi Lab

2 The Morton Arboretum

3 Historic Geneva

4 The Hindu Temple of Greater Chicago

BBGB BREWERY & HOP FARM

FIELD NOTES

200 W. Orchard Rd.
North Aurora, IL
60542
630-299-3977
eathardware.com

Sustainability practices are the name of the game for BBGB, with spent grain from the brewery being used for the restaurant's pizza dough, dinner rolls, slider buns, and dog treats. Decor and architecture is all reused/recycled/ salvaged (railroad ties, re-purposed glass, whiskey barrels, etc.). There's also a green wall at the entrance, regulating temperature for the building, and providing a lovely, almost rainforest sort of vibe on the outside of this suburban destination. The plan is to have the 1.5-acre hop farm generate 80% of the brewery's hops.

OWNER
Bruce Burns, Brent Fiedor

HEAD BREWER
Brent Fiedor

AVAILABILITY
Chicago - limited draft only

BEST KNOWN FOR
IPAs, saisons, dark ales

DATE FOUNDED
2016

2016 PRODUCTION
N/A

20 | 210 | • | | | • | | | • | • | | 3.6/5

BBGB BREWERY & HOP FARM

PRO TIPS

» Brewery tours do not need to be scheduled, but rather a friendly manager or brewer can take your group on a tour with a simple ask.

» Tours feature not just the brewery, but also the hop farm, greenhouse, and other sustainability practices that BBGB undertakes.

» Most meats are smoked and cured in-house too, featuring a brisket hot dog and charcuterie plates of various sizes.

» Food from Hardware (the name of the restaurant adjacent to the taproom) can be ordered in the taproom.

» For fans of brown liquor, Hardware offers over 350 whiskey selections.

POPULAR BEERS

Earl The Pearl

Barney's Coffee Stout

Butch's Badass Porter

DATE OF VISIT:

MY RATING
☆ ☆ ☆ ☆ ☆

NOTES:

M	Tu	W	Th	F	S	Su
closed	11a-10p	11a-10p	11a-10p	11a-12a	11a-12a	12p-9p

DRY CITY BREW WORKS

FIELD NOTES

120B N. Main St.
Wheaton, IL 60187
630-456-4787
**drycitybrewworks.
com**

With over 70 churches in the area, plus the presence of evangelical Wheaton College, Wheaton is regarded as one of Chicago's more conservative suburbs. There's even a rumor that the 80s film Footloose was based on the small city. Liquor sales in restaurants weren't opened up until 1985, but the craft beer boom has led to this suburb opening up a brewpub. Dry City plays on this history, not only in its name, but in the speakeasy-esque side entrance to the taproom itself. While Dry City could get by merely on its back-story, they take their beer seriously too.

OWNER
Ben Sampson,
Jessica Sampson,
David Carr, Lori Carr

HEAD BREWER
Ben Sampson

AVAILABILITY
Taproom and limited
local restaurants

BEST KNOWN FOR
Stouts, red ales

DATE FOUNDED
2014

2016 PRODUCTION
400 bbl

PUBLIC TRANSIT
UP-W/Wheaton

6 | 25 | • | • | • | | • | | | • | • | 4.0/5

DRY CITY BREW WORKS

PRO TIPS

» Located on a quaint main street in an area that screams small-town Midwestern America, this classy taproom sports exposed brick and classy, wooden furniture that helps to modernize, but also shouts out the past of the building. Edison bulbs hang above, and pressed tin tiles are tacked underneath the bar.

» Wheaton only permits 3 servings (1 serving = 1 pint or flight) of alcohol per person per day, so plan accordingly.

» Local musicians will sometimes play on Fridays and Saturdays.

» Taproom is small, but they do have some outdoor seating.

» Credit cards only.

DATE OF VISIT:

MY RATING
☆ ☆ ☆ ☆ ☆

NOTES:

POPULAR BEERS

Kilty Plea	Light as the Breeze	Rocket Fuel Rye	Stout-Man

M	Tu	W	Th	F	S	Su
closed	closed	4p-9p	4p-9p	3p-10p	2p-10p	2p-6p

HOPVINE BREWING CO.

FIELD NOTES

4030 Fox Valley
Center Dr.
Aurora, IL 60504
630-229-6030
**hopvinebrewing-
company.com**

Opened in October 2013, Hopvine is located in an a strip mall close to the Fox Valley Mall and just a short drive from the famous Aurora Outlet Mall. Husband and wife team, Jan and Doug Isley, had previously worked in the beer industry before opening up Hopvine. It's a family-run business and focuses on craft beer as well as an extensive food menu. While they have a long bar that is great if you want to grab a quick drink, if you want to settle down, order some food and listen to the live music they have on the weekends they also have a large area with tables.

OWNER
Doug Isley, Jan Isley

HEAD BREWER
Ken McMullen

AVAILABILITY
Limited local draft
only

BEST KNOWN FOR
Wheat ales, red/
brown ales

DATE FOUNDED
2013

2016 PRODUCTION
158 bbl

| 32 | 277 | • | | • | • | | • | • | | 3.5/5 |

HOPVINE BREWING CO.

PRO TIPS

» They have a big menu that features sandwiches, wraps, and small plates.

» Chef driven food made from scratch creates a unique intimacy between their beer and menu selections. They have their own garden and even grow some hops.

» Always have two craft sodas available.

» Live music on Saturdays - it can get loud so if you prefer a quiet setting, go before the music.

» Happy hour is from 4-7p everyday they are open.

DATE OF VISIT:

MY RATING
☆ ☆ ☆ ☆ ☆

NOTES:

POPULAR BEERS

| Brew Monkey | Urban Tumble-weed | Mast-odon | Aurora Amber Ale |

M	Tu	W	Th	F	S	Su
closed	4p-10p	4p-10p	11a-11p	11a-12a	11a-12a	11a-9p

METAL MONKEY BREWING

FIELD NOTES

Metal Monkey's logo is a pretty good look into their ethos. It's a consternated-looking simian flashing double devil-horn signs with its hands toward the viewer. One doubts that they are going to find a bevy of understated beers and session ales here. The stated goal of Metal Monkey "is to make kick ass craft beer." A mix of style reverence and experimentation informs the progress toward the stated goal, as does access to barrels and plenty of hops, of course.

515 Anderson Dr.
Romeoville, IL
60446
815-524-3139
metalmonkeybrew-ing.com

OWNER
Brett & Rachel Smith, Dan & Brandi Camp, Jason Janes

HEAD BREWER
Dan Camp, Jason Janes

AVAILABILITY
Very limited - draft only

BEST KNOWN FOR
Wheat ales, stouts, pales, IPAs

DATE FOUNDED
2016

2016 PRODUCTION
400 bbl

KEY EVENTS
Bourbon Barrel-Aged Stout bottle release (winter)

16 | 90 | | | • | • | | | | • | | 4.0/5

METAL MONKEY BREWING

PRO TIPS

» Producing less than 500 barrels a year, Metal Monkey currently only serves its beer out of its space, save for a couple neighborhood spots around Romeoville.

» There's some barstool seating, but the tables and overstuffed couches more than make up for any shortage there.

» Plenty of board games available for patrons to enjoy while having their brews.

» Bottle releases take place only occasionally, so if you're interested in that, check ahead of time.

» Typically schedules lots of food trucks.

DATE OF VISIT:

MY RATING
☆ ☆ ☆ ☆ ☆

NOTES:

POPULAR BEERS

Fonkey Mucker	Tony's Car	Simian Fever	Asmo- deus

M	Tu	W	Th	F	S	Su
12p-9p	closed	closed	12p-9p	12p-11p	12p-11p	12p-9p

NEVIN'S BREWING COMPANY

FIELD NOTES

12337 South Rte 59
Plainfield, IL 60585
815-436-3900
nevinsbrewing.com

A lot of breweries tout their game when it comes to being sustainable or green, and not in the Kermit the Frog way. Nevin's boasts of the brewery's donation of its spent grain to local farmers, not just for feed use, but also for composting and soil enrichment. The steaks, burgers, salads, and sides at Nevin's all benefit from this sort of circle of life. Like many other suburban destinations, you'll find some styles for craft beer initiates, including a pilsner, a Märzen, a Belgian witbier, and a pale ale, but you can also find a caramelly rich doppelbock, an imperial IPA, and an imperial red.

OWNER
Nevin's Restaurant Group

HEAD BREWER
Marc Wilson

AVAILABILITY
Limited draft only

BEST KNOWN FOR
Stouts, Belgians, lagers

DATE FOUNDED
2013

2016 PRODUCTION
429 bbl

RECENT AWARDS
GABF 2016

20 | 300 | • | | • | • | | • | • | | 3.2/5

NEVIN'S BREWING COMPANY

PRO TIPS

» Nevin's boasts perhaps the most encyclopedic wing menu of any brewpub in the city, featuring bone-in, boneless, and tenders options, plus your choice of over a dozen different sauces, and your choice of different "dusts." Try one of five different dressings on the side to cool off.

» Nevin's features local live music (sometimes with a cover) on most weekend nights.

» Host a trivia night on most Wednesdays.

» Food and drink specials on Sundays and Tuesday to Thursday.

» When there's a big game on, they'll have it on at the taproom.

DATE OF VISIT:

MY RATING
☆ ☆ ☆ ☆ ☆

NOTES:

POPULAR BEERS

| South Side Stout | Kookie Monster | Quick Witted | Wishful Thinking |

M	Tu	W	Th	F	S	Su
closed	3p-1a	3p-1a	3p-1a	3p-2a	11:30-2	11:30-12

PENROSE BREWING COMPANY

FIELD NOTES

509 Stevens St.
Geneva, IL 60134
630-232-2115
**penrosebrewing.
com**

Head Brewer Tom Korder founded Penrose after his departure from Goose Island in 2013. The focus of Penrose is Belgian-inspired ales with an accent on sessionability and wild fermentation. Expect a couple IPAs, a sour or two, and several Belgians on tap when you go. It's obvious that Korder loves working with various flavors, fermenting organisms, and aging methods with his beers. He gives them the time that they need and the results are justification for the time and effort spent.

OWNER
Tom Korder

HEAD BREWER
Tom Korder

AVAILABILITY
Chicago

BEST KNOWN FOR
Belgians, sours,
pales, IPAs

DATE FOUNDED
2014

2016 PRODUCTION
3,000 bbl

KEY EVENTS
Bottle releases for
wild series

PUBLIC TRANSIT
UP-W/Geneva

15 | 105 | | | • | | | | • | • | 3.9/5

PENROSE BREWING COMPANY

PRO TIPS

» Bottle releases usually generate sizable lines, so if you're headed to one of these, make sure you dress for the weather and allow yourself plenty of time.

» Expect plenty of variety and a special beer or two on tap any time you go. Many of their beers don't get distribution. You can only try them at the taproom or by filling up your growler.

» Penrose's "Ten Buck Tour" gets you a beer and a glass you can keep; tours are available Friday, Saturday, and Sunday, and can be booked online.

» Taproom is credit card only.

» Food trucks will show up periodically, but you can also bring your own food.

DATE OF VISIT:

MY RATING
☆ ☆ ☆ ☆ ☆

NOTES:

POPULAR BEERS

M	Tu	W	Th	F	S	Su
1p-9p	1p-9p	1p-9p	1p-9p	1p-10p	11a-10p	11a-6p

SOLEMN OATH BREWERY

FIELD NOTES

Heavy metal imagery and intimidating label art (including beer names like Pain Cave, Wreckage Master, Death by Viking, and Punk Rock for Rich Kids) obscures the delicious and drinkable brews of this Naperville brewery. Brothers John and Joe Barley (what a great last name for a brewer) opened Solemn Oath in 2012 after hosting a tasting with friends. Their focus is on West Coast, Belgian, and barrel-aged beers, but that doesn't stop them from making a mean Kölsch (Lü), or experimenting with other styles.

1661 Quincy Ave.
Naperville, IL 60540
630-995-3062
**solemnoathbrewery.
com**

OWNER
John Barley

HEAD BREWER
Tim Marshall

AVAILABILITY
Chicago, WI

BEST KNOWN FOR
IPAs, hoppy reds,
Belgians, Kölsch

DATE FOUNDED
2012

2016 PRODUCTION
4,217 bbl

RECENT AWARDS
GABF 2016

KEY EVENTS
Oath Day (Jun)

10 | 80 | | | • | | | • | | 3.9/5

SOLEMN OATH BREWERY

PRO TIPS

» A half wall divides the brewing quarters from the taproom space, allowing guests the chance to see the process in all its glory.

» The "Oath Day" anniversary party every June is a large affair featuring food trucks, out-of-rotation beers, and general mayhem.

» Three beer limit per day (local law).

» The Old Order club is a great way to get access to exclusive events, beer releases and a lot more. Cost for 2017 was $195.

» Current taproom is quite small but there are plans to take over an adjoining space in the future to allow for a larger taproom.

» Credit card only and no tips.

DATE OF VISIT:

MY RATING
☆ ☆ ☆ ☆ ☆

NOTES:

POPULAR BEERS

M	Tu	W	Th	F	S	Su
12p-9p	12p-9p	12p-9p	12p-9p	11a-11p	11a-11p	11a-7p

TWO BROTHERS ARTISAN BREWING

FIELD NOTES

30W315 Calumet Ave. W
Warrenville, IL 60555
630-393-2337
**twobrothersbrewing.
com**

Two Brothers maintains four spaces in the Chicago area, as well as one in Scottsdale, AZ. Started in 1996 by Jim and Jason Ebel, the original location for Two Brothers is in a Warrenville warehouse and the location we chose to feature in this guide (after all, it's the granddaddy). In 2011, the Ebels purchased the roundhouse in Aurora, IL formerly owned by Walter Payton. The third, called The Craftsman, does not feature a brewery, but opened as a market/tavern hybrid in 2016. And the fourth just opened in 2017 in the heart of Oak Park as a restaurant/espresso bar.

OWNER
Jim Ebel, Jason Ebel

HEAD BREWER
Jeremy Bogan

AVAILABILITY
IL, AZ, CT, FL, IA,
IN, MD, MO, NJ, NY,
OH, WI

BEST KNOWN FOR
Pales, IPAs, Belgians,
sours

DATE FOUNDED
1996

2016 PRODUCTION
37,500 bbl

RECENT AWARDS
GABF 2016, WBC
2016, FoBAB 2016

KEY EVENTS
Two Brothers
Festival (Jun)

18 | 250 | • | | • | • | | • | • | | 3.8/5

TWO BROTHERS ARTISAN BREWING

PRO TIPS

» The original Warrenville Tap House has more of a standard suburban brewpub atmosphere, and features fewer entrées on the food menu. But there's a pizza oven that allows guests to craft their own 10" pies.

» Brewery tours are available at this location; they're free and on Saturday afternoons. Reservations are available online.

» Homebrew shop is connected to the taproom. You can find everything you need to brew your own beer here including equipment and ingredients.

» If you can make it a double stop trip, head to The Roundhouse in Aurora, a former railway building that is impressive in itself. The 1856 building is 70,000 square feet.

DATE OF VISIT:

MY RATING
☆ ☆ ☆ ☆ ☆

NOTES:

POPULAR BEERS

M	Tu	W	Th	F	S	Su
11a-11p	11a-11p	11a-11p	11a-11p	11a-12a	11a-12a	11a-9p

WERK FORCE BREWING CO.

FIELD NOTES

14903 S. Center St.
Plainfield, IL 60544
815-531-5557
**werkforcebrewing.
com**

This nanobrewery in Plainfield makes use of the resources available at its sister homebrew shop, Chicago Brew Werks, such as experimental ingredients and yeast strains to create continuously new and risky beers. Wild, sour, and fruit-infused beers are a main feature of Werk Force, which still doesn't eschew keeping a hoppy option and a stout on tap. With the entire resources of a massive homebrew store at their disposal, one can only feel like the brewers at Werk Force are children working at the candy store, or DJs working at the record store.

OWNER
Brandon Wright,
Amanda Wright

HEAD BREWER
Steve Woertendyke

AVAILABILITY
Limited local

BEST KNOWN FOR
IPAs, pales, saisons

DATE FOUNDED
2014

2016 PRODUCTION
475 bbl

RECENT AWARDS
FoBAB 2016

KEY EVENTS
Anniversary Party
(Jun)

13 | 50 | | • | • | | • | | | • | | 4.3/5

WERK FORCE BREWING CO.

PRO TIPS

» It's not often that you get a world-class homebrew shop (the largest in the Midwest) next to, or practically within, your taproom, so definitely check the Chicago Brew Werks store out and see if the homebrew bug bites you.

» There's no kitchen, but food trucks will come by.

» There are no stools at the bar, but you're more than welcome to stand there with your beverage. There are also barrels for folks to gather around.

» A larger taproom expected to open sometime in 2017.

DATE OF VISIT:

MY RATING
☆ ☆ ☆ ☆ ☆

NOTES:

POPULAR BEERS

| The Beer Formerly Known As... | Oats Made Me Do It | Farm-house Vultures | Pressure Drop |

M	Tu	W	Th	F	S	Su
closed	10a-7p	10a-7p	10a-7p	10a-7p	10a-5p	12p-3p

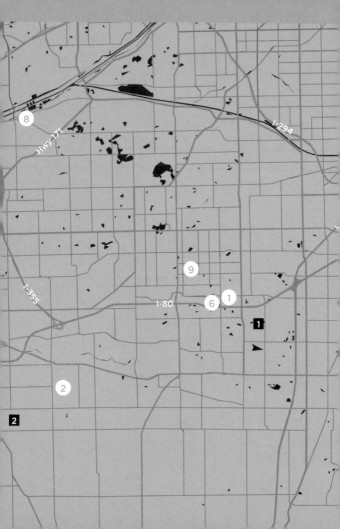

SUBURBS SOUTH

1. 350 Brewing Co.
2. Arrowhead Ales Brewing Company
3. Blue Island Beer Co.
4. Evil Horse Brewing Co.
5. Flossmoor Station
6. Hailstorm Brewing Co.
7. One Trick Pony
8. Pollyanna Brewing Company
9. Tribes Beer Company

I-294

Hwy 1

NEIGHBORHOOD HIGHLIGHTS

1 Hollywood Casino Amphitheatre

2 Chicagoland Speedway

3 Original Rainbow Cone

4 Balmoral Racing Club

350 BREWING CO.

FIELD NOTES

350 was the street number of this brewing company's founders when they were undergraduates at Northern Illinois. Todd Randall and Erik Pizer (now head brewer at Rock Bottom in Warrenville, IL) were known to undertake dubious projects in their college days, including a nascent wrestling federation and punk bands based out of their attic. After Erik moved on to graduate school and Todd to a corporate job, the temptation for more crazy ideas continued until 2013 when they started 350 Brewing, likely one of their least dubious projects.

7144 183rd St.
Tinley Park, IL 60477
708-825-7339
350brewing.com

OWNER
Todd Randall

HEAD BREWER
Dusty Peters

AVAILABILITY
Taproom only

BEST KNOWN FOR
IPAs, lighter styles

DATE FOUNDED
2013

2016 PRODUCTION
380 bbl

KEY EVENTS
350 Fest (Aug)

20 | 120 | | | • | • | | • | • | | 3.9/5

350 BREWING CO.

PRO TIPS

» August 2017 will mark the third iteration of 350 Fest, a brewery-run annual party hosted at the Tinley Park Convention Center. The festival combines 350's beer and punk and ska bands for a full day of mayhem and delight.

» The appetizer menu is filled with fried items, including wings, cheese sticks, fried dough, even avocado. Sandwiches include a burger, chicken, pot roast, BBQ pork, and an open-faced burger with fries slathered in cheese sauce called The Southside 'Shoe. Go big or go home.

» Very close to the Hollywood Casino Amphitheatre. Great place to go before or after a concert.

DATE OF VISIT:

MY RATING

NOTES:

POPULAR BEERS

| Crook County IPA | Howdy Neighbor | Stupid Kid | I Hate Mondays |

M	Tu	W	Th	F	S	Su
12p-10p	12p-10p	12p-10p	12p-10p	12p-12a	12p-12a	12p-8p

ARROWHEAD ALES BREWING COMPANY

FIELD NOTES

New Lenox is closer to Joliet than it is to Chicago, but if you find yourself on the far southwestern side of the metro area, check out this 200-person restaurant/brewery. Founder and head brewer Mike Bacon's journey to craft beer is a well-trod story: sit in on some homebrewing sessions hosted by friends; research styles and the science behind making great beer; get homebrew set-up; hone your recipes; develop a pathological desire to share your creations with others; and voilà you can start a brewery. It's just that easy.

2010 Calistoga Dr.
New Lenox, IL 60451
815-717-6068
arrowheadales.com

OWNER
Mike Bacon

HEAD BREWER
Mike Bacon

AVAILABILITY
Chicago - limited distribution

BEST KNOWN FOR
Stouts, IPAs

DATE FOUNDED
2016

2016 PRODUCTION
245 bbl

PUBLIC TRANSIT
SWS/Laraway Rd.

| 12 | 200 | • | | • | • | | • | • | • | 3.8/5 |

ARROWHEAD ALES BREWING COMPANY

PRO TIPS

» Arrowhead's friendly suburban brick architecture houses an inviting atmosphere, and a spacious interior.

» For a suburban brewpub with the usual pizzas, appetizers, and burgers, there's a surprising level of experimentation with many options on the menu.

» The SMASH series features brews made with a single malt and single hop variety. It's a great way to explore the flavor capabilities of different component ingredients in beer.

» Live music is hosted several times each month, as well as Open Mic nights and beer education classes. Check Facebook posts for dates.

DATE OF VISIT:

MY RATING

☆ ☆ ☆ ☆ ☆

NOTES:

POPULAR BEERS

Devil's Break-fast	Weed Wacker	Coconut Killjoy	Entry Level Snob

M	Tu	W	Th	F	S	Su
11a-10p	11a-10p	11a-10p	11a-10p	11a-1a	11a-1a	11a-10p

BLUE ISLAND BEER CO.

FIELD NOTES

13357 Old Western
Blue Island, IL
60406
708-954-8085
**blueislandbeerco.
com**

Head brewer Bryan Shimkos has produced some truly great beers for a few different Chicago-area breweries, including Flossmoor Station and the now-defunct Ale Syndicate, before striking out on his own with this south suburban project just south of the Little Calumet River. His experiments with barrel-aging earned him a stellar reputation among those in-the-know with Chicago craft beer, and he brings that expertise to Blue Island. Expect a decent range of American-style beers with a healthy dose of hearty IPAs and stouts.

OWNER
Bryan Shimkos, Alan
Cromwell

HEAD BREWER
Bryan Shimkos

AVAILABILITY
Chicago

BEST KNOWN FOR
Stouts, IPAs,
sessionable ales

DATE FOUNDED
2015

2016 PRODUCTION
367 bbl

KEY EVENTS
Uprising Craft
Market (Apr, Dec)

PUBLIC TRANSIT
RI/Blue Island-
Vermont, ME/Blue
Island

12 | 56 | | • | • | • | • | • | | • | • | 4.0/5

BLUE ISLAND BEER CO.

PRO TIPS

» Food trucks will be by occasionally, but you can also bring your own food.

» They have a couple arcade games for those who want to occupy themselves while standing.

» Music events are a big part of Blue Island. Live music acts perform occasionally, but customers can get in on the act, too. Mandolinist Steve Haberichter hosts a monthly bluegrass jam on the first Wednesday of the month, while the "What the Folk?" song circle encourages guests to bring a potluck dish along with their instrument.

DATE OF VISIT:

MY RATING
☆ ☆ ☆ ☆ ☆

NOTES:

POPULAR BEERS

M	Tu	W	Th	F	S	Su
closed	2p-9p	2p-9p	2p-9p	2p-10p	12p-10p	12p-6p

EVIL HORSE BREWING CO.

FIELD NOTES

1338 Main St.
Crete, IL 60417
708-304-2907
**evilhorsebrewing.
com**

In the far-south suburb of Crete you will find Evil Horse Brewing. Brewmaster Steve Kamp has been homebrewing since the 1980s, even serving as president of the Chicago Beer Society, a group of area beer enthusiasts that's been around as long as craft beer has been in Chicago. After receiving his education from Siebel and Doemens, and assisting at Brickstone, Flossmoor Station and Lagunitas, Kamp's got his own thing now. Sharing a name with his Evil Horse Farm, Kamp's beers represent a wide range of brewing styles from light lagers to barrel-aged stouts.

OWNER
Pinsetter Brands

HEAD BREWER
Steve Kamp

AVAILABILITY
IL

BEST KNOWN FOR
Pales, dark ales, wheat ales

DATE FOUNDED
2015

2016 PRODUCTION
377 bbl

KEY EVENTS
Anniversary Party (Apr), Downtown Hottie Days (Jun)

14 | 150 | • | • | • | • | | | • | | 3.8/5

EVIL HORSE BREWING CO.

PRO TIPS

» Remember the volcano in Iceland whose eruption in 2010 disrupted air travel all over Europe? Evil Horse named their Barrel-Aged Imperial Stout after it. It's called Eyjafjallajökull (AY-ya-FYAHD-la-JOO-kull-[tongue click]). You can also just call it "barrel-aged imperial stout" but it's up to you.

» The taproom mixes the atmosphere of an English pub with a small-town neighborhood gathering place.

» There's no kitchen at the taproom, but food trucks will come by occasionally.

» Brewery tours are on some Saturdays, but not all; call in advance.

» They're known for having fun events throughout the week like trivia, bingo and Euchre.

DATE OF VISIT:

MY RATING
☆ ☆ ☆ ☆ ☆

NOTES:

POPULAR BEERS

| | | Eyjafjal-lajökull | Paxon The Ponyless |

M	Tu	W	Th	F	S	Su
closed	3p-11p	3p-11p	3p-11p	3p-12a	12p-12a	closed

FLOSSMOOR STATION

FIELD NOTES

Quite possibly the first train station turned into a brewery in the Chicagoland area (beating out the roundhouse in Aurora that now carries the Two Brothers name). Flossmoor Station has been around since 1996, ancient by craft beer standards. But don't let their 20 years of experience fool you though. Flossmoor was named best small brewery in America at the 2006 Great American Beer Festival, and have continued to win prestigious awards for their beers since then, over 80 in total.

1035 Sterling Ave.
Flossmoor, IL 60422
708-957-2739
**flossmoorstation.
com**

OWNER
Dean Armstrong,
Carolyn Armstrong

HEAD BREWER
Ryan Czaja

AVAILABILITY
Brewpub only

BEST KNOWN FOR
IPAs, brown/amber
ales, barrel-aged
beers

DATE FOUNDED
1996

2016 PRODUCTION
600 bbl

KEY EVENTS
Pre-Dark Lord
Day (Apr/May),
Oktoberfest (Sept)

PUBLIC TRANSIT
ME/Flossmoor

16	240	•		•	•		•		•	3.8/5

FLOSSMOOR STATION

PRO TIPS

» Though the brewpub is in an old, unused train station, across the street you'll find the Metra line that can take you directly north into downtown Chicago.

» Free happy hour buffet Friday 4-6p with a drink purchase.

» The woodgrain on the inside and outside gives a vibe somewhere between vintage train station, a German beer hall, and an upscale Midwestern family restaurant.

» Menu theme is "gourmet pub food," with sandwiches, BBQ, shared appetizers, and a cheese and charcuterie plate.

» Bombers of special releases are sometimes available at the brewery.

DATE OF VISIT:

MY RATING
☆ ☆ ☆ ☆ ☆

NOTES:

POPULAR BEERS

M	Tu	W	Th	F	S	Su
11:30-11	11:30-11	11:30-11	11:30-11	11:30-11	11:30-12	11:30-12

HAILSTORM BREWING CO.

FIELD NOTES

8060 W. 186th St.
Tinley Park, IL
60487
708-480-2268
**hailstormbrewing.
com**

Since 2014, this Tinley Park brewery has gained fans for some of the most extreme beers made in the Chicago area. Their Vlad series of imperial stouts sees a massive number of permutations and reinterpretations with all sorts of adjuncts (coconut, raspberry, vanilla, etc.) and barrel-agings. They were one of the first Chicagoland breweries to try their hand at the hazy, buzzy New England-style IPA, which is known for not being too bitter, but heavily dry-hopped and left unfiltered for huge notes of orange juice and sweet citrus.

OWNER
Brandon Banbury,
Chris Schiller, Gene
Wabisczewicz, Josh
Wabisczewicz

HEAD BREWER
Brandon Banbury

AVAILABILITY
Chicago

BEST KNOWN FOR
NE IPAs, stouts

DATE FOUNDED
2014

2016 PRODUCTION
1,622 bbl

RECENT AWARDS
FoBAB 2016, GABF
2015

KEY EVENTS
Anniversary Party
(Apr)

| 16 | 200 | | | • | • | | | | • | | 4.1/5 |

HAILSTORM BREWING CO.

PRO TIPS

» The Tasting Room shares a space with the impressively-sized production space, featuring barrels stacked as many as six high.

» Go during nice weather if you want to get some natural light from the open garage door.

» If you're looking for a session brew, this probably isn't your destination.

» Close to 350 Brewing and the Hollywood Casino Amphiteatre.

» Open Mic Night on Thursdays. Live music, as well as food trucks on Fridays and Saturdays.

» For their special third anniversary release, they're even trying their hand at a wild-fermented raspberry lambic.

DATE OF VISIT:

MY RATING

NOTES:

POPULAR BEERS

M	Tu	W	Th	F	S	Su
closed	12p-8p	12p-8p	12p-8p	12p-10p	12p-10p	12p-8p

ONE TRICK PONY

FIELD NOTES

One Trick Pony

17933 Chappel Ave.
Lansing, IL 60438
708-889-6683
**onetrickponybrew-
ery.co**

With a mascot featuring a horse sporting a monstrously-toothy grin, One Trick Pony is one of those places that you don't have to worry if they're taking themselves too seriously or not. Out of the southern suburb of Lansing, their website is quick to level with the reader: "Our beer won't make you strong or handsome, but if you appreciate craft beer and want to meet some guys that are happy to make it, serve it, and probably drink it with you, stop by or give us a call." That sort of honesty is appreciated in craft beer these days.

OWNER
Mark Kocol

HEAD BREWER
Jonathan Hickey

AVAILABILITY
Chicago, NW IN

BEST KNOWN FOR
IPAs, red ales,
hefeweizens, stouts

DATE FOUNDED
2011

2016 PRODUCTION
670 bbl

| 24 | 50 | • | • | • | • | • | | • | | 4.1/5 |

ONE TRICK PONY

PRO TIPS

» The space is warm and inviting, with strings of exposed bulbs lighting the cinder block and wood-adorned space, letting you see their downright insane collection of vintage wooden beer boxes, growlers and other bottles lining the walls.

» During nice weather, the patio seating area is almost garden-like.

» Firkin Fridays let the taproom feature a cask-conditioned real ale to celebrate the end of the week.

» Bands will sometimes crowd into the corner to play live, but call in advance to see when the next artist is scheduled.

DATE OF VISIT:

MY RATING
☆ ☆ ☆ ☆ ☆

NOTES:

POPULAR BEERS

  Warlander Marsh Tacky

M	Tu	W	Th	F	S	Su
6p-11p	3p-11p	3p-11p	3p-11p	3p-11p	3p-11p	2p-10p

POLLYANNA BREWING COMPANY

FIELD NOTES

431 Talcott Ave.
Lemont, IL 60439
630-914-5834
**pollyannabrewing.
com**

Pollyanna's main aim for their beers is balance, be it a raspberry-accented German hefeweizen (Summerly), a perfectly tuned Midwest style IPA (Lexical Gap), or a barrel-aged stout with wild yeast (Ernest 1953). There will be something for everyone at this lovely and impressively-sized brewery in Lemont, IL. Mazzie (pronounced MAY-zee) pale ale references Mazzie's Place, a 1890's-era establishment in Pollyanna's hometown of Lemont that offered its patrons some creature comforts in life; namely, it offered booze, gambling, and female companionship.

OWNER
Brian Pawola, Ed Malner, Paul Ciciora, Don Ciciora, Ryan Weidner

HEAD BREWER
Brian Pawola

AVAILABILITY
IL

BEST KNOWN FOR
IPAs, pales, lighter ales, Belgians, Germans

DATE FOUNDED
2013

2016 PRODUCTION
1,926 bbl

RECENT AWARDS
GABF 2016

KEY EVENTS
Berries & Bros (Apr), Beer Fest (Jun), Oktoberfest (Sept), Anniv. Party (Oct)

PUBLIC TRANSIT
HC/Lemont

| 12 | 46 | • | | • | | • | | • | | | • | | • | | 3.9/5 |

POLLYANNA BREWING COMPANY

PRO TIPS

» Dog friendly on the patio only.

» Their Berries and Bros Block Party in April celebrates the yearly release of Summerly, the raspberry wheat ale that's become one of Pollyanna's best sellers.

» The taproom itself is inviting, well-lit, and stylish, with about a dozen bar seats and some hi-top tables. Ample patio seating overlooking the nearby waterway is also available, weather permitting.

» Tours are available during cold-weather months on Fridays and Saturdays with reservations available online.

» Live music and food trucks generally on Fridays.

POPULAR BEERS

M	Tu	W	Th	F	S	Su
closed	3p-10p	3p-10p	3p-10p	3p-11p	12p-11p	12p-7p

DATE OF VISIT:

MY RATING

☆ ☆ ☆ ☆ ☆

NOTES:

TRIBES BEER COMPANY

FIELD NOTES

11220 W. Lincoln Hwy
Mokena, IL 60448
815-464-0248
**tribesbeercompany.
com**

With locations in both Mokena and Tinley Park, Tribes is quickly making their mark on the brewpub scene in the southwestern suburbs. Both locations had been open as restaurants for quite awhile (Mokena in 2009, Tinley Park in 2012) before the idea to start the Tribes Beer Company came to fruition in 2015. A 7-barrel system with six fermenters allows for a decent amount of Tribes-made beer to invade the taps at their locations. The focus may be on hop-forward brews, but that doesn't preclude head brewer David Kerns from making beers that are all over the map.

OWNER
Niall Freyne

HEAD BREWER
David Kerns

AVAILABILITY
IL - draft only

BEST KNOWN FOR
IPAs, pales, Kölsch

DATE FOUNDED
2009

2016 PRODUCTION
620 bbl

KEY EVENTS
Tribes Beer Fest
(Jul)

42 | 150 | • | | | • | • | | • | • | | 3.9/5

TRIBES BEER COMPANY

PRO TIPS

» The Mokena location features 38 different drafts with over a dozen being house-made, while Tinley Park has 52 options, including up to 10 Tribes brands.

» For food options, you can start by crafting your own meat and cheese plate, or getting some mussels or the poutine of the day. Entrées and sandwiches are fairly by-the-book, but the Korean short rib tacos are good at any hour.

» A production brewery that will have its own taproom is in the works for 2018.

» Team trivia on Mondays and taco specials on Tuesdays.

» Close to the Hollywood Casino Amphitheater.

DATE OF VISIT:

MY RATING
☆ ☆ ☆ ☆ ☆

NOTES:

POPULAR BEERS

Big Twin Double IPA | O To 100 | Lincoln-Way Red Rye | Double IPA

M	Tu	W	Th	F	S	Su
11:30-12	11:30-12	11:30-1a	11:30-1a	11:30-1a	11:30-1a	11:30-12

SUBURBS NORTHWEST INDIANA

1. 18th Street Brewery
2. 3 Floyds Brewing Co.
3. Bulldog Brewing Co.
4. Byway Brewing
5. The Devil's Trumpet Brewing Co.
6. New Oberpfalz Brewing
7. Pokro Brewing Company
8. St. John Malt Brothers Craft Brewers
9. Wildrose Brewing
10. Windmill Brewing

NEIGHBORHOOD HIGHLIGHTS

1 Gary SouthShore RailCats

2 Indiana Dunes National Lakeshore

3 Albanese Candy Factory

4 Horseshoe Hammond

18TH STREET BREWERY

FIELD NOTES

Drew Fox's career in craft beer started with a trip to Belgium more than a decade ago. After time spent at Half Acre and Pipeworks, Fox started brewing under the 18th Street name (the street in Chicago's Pilsen neighborhood where the idea for the brewery first came to Fox) via contract at Pipeworks and Spiteful. A successful Kickstarter campaign in 2012 led to the opening of a brewery and taproom in Gary, IN. Since then, a Hammond location has followed, as well as large amounts of well-deserved acclaim.

5725 Miller Ave.
Gary, IN 46403
219-939-8802
**18thstreetbrewery.
com**

OWNER
Drew Fox

HEAD BREWER
Drew Fox

AVAILABILITY
Chicago, NW IN

BEST KNOWN FOR
Imp. IPAs, pales, stouts

DATE FOUNDED
2012

2016 PRODUCTION
1,250 bbl

RECENT AWARDS
FoBAB 2016

KEY EVENTS
Barrel Massacre (varied dates)

PUBLIC TRANSIT
South Shore/Gary

9 | 60 | | | • | | • | • | • | 4.0/5

18TH STREET BREWERY

PRO TIPS

» The Gary taproom has a smaller menu focused on perfect-for-lunch sandwiches and bar snacks. The Hammond brewpub's menu is larger.

» The rare barrel-aged bottle offering might be available, but be sure to check their regularly updated online list.

» All packaged beers sell quickly, so don't expect something you see today to be there tomorrow.

» Although 18th Street doesn't quite yet have the buzz or the cache of it's close neighbor 3 Floyds, it's certainly well on its way there.

» They do a ton of beer and food pairings throughout the year.

» Known for their artwork by Joey Potts.

DATE OF VISIT:

MY RATING
☆ ☆ ☆ ☆ ☆

NOTES:

POPULAR BEERS

M	Tu	W	Th	F	S	Su
closed	2p-10p	2p-10p	2p-10p	12p-11p	12p-11p	12p-6p

3 FLOYDS BREWING CO.

FIELD NOTES

9750 Indiana Pkwy.
Munster, IN 46321
219-922-4425
3floyds.com

Founded in 1996, 3 Floyds is notorious for being rated as one of the Chicago area's best and most sought-after breweries. Their unassuming location, in a suburban office park still doesn't obscure that this metal-themed brewpub and brewery makes some serious beer in their own, idiosyncratic way. The Floyd brothers cut their teeth on hoppy, attitudinal beers that are hop forward, but still extremely approachable. They are also known for Dark Lord, a massive Russian Imperial Stout brewed with Dark Matter Coffee that is only available once a year during their ticketed event.

OWNER
Nick Floyd

HEAD BREWER
Chris Boggess

AVAILABILITY
IL, IN, WI, OH, KY

BEST KNOWN FOR
Pales, IPAs, imp. stouts

DATE FOUNDED
1996

2016 PRODUCTION
55,248 bbl

RECENT AWARDS
WBC 2016

KEY EVENTS
Dark Lord Day (Apr/May)

20	75				•				•	•		3.9/5

3 FLOYDS BREWING CO.

PRO TIPS

» The space is small, with metal music usually blaring. The place may seem intimidating or off-putting, even during a weekday lunch, but at the end of the day it's just a brewpub with excellent beers run by a bunch of metal-heads.

» The place's reputation precedes it, so expect a wait.

» There's a beer-to-go and a merchandise kiosk next to the pub. But don't expect to be able to get a case of Zombie Dust, or a bottle of the latest barrel-aged release whenever you go.

» As for the food, it's chef-driven pub fare with plenty to choose from, and nary a bum pick among the options.

» Just added Todd Haug from Surly heritage to their NW Indiana team.

POPULAR BEERS

DATE OF VISIT:

MY RATING
☆ ☆ ☆ ☆ ☆

NOTES:

M	Tu	W	Th	F	S	Su
11-11:15p	11-11:15p	11-11:15p	11-11:15p	11-1:15a	11-1:15a	11-11:15p

BULLDOG BREWING CO.

FIELD NOTES

1409 119th St.
Whiting, IN 46394
219-655-5284
**bulldogbrewingco.
com**

Brewmaster Kevin Clark and co-owner Jeff Kochis are both originally from northwest Indiana, and have come together to bring a welcoming, neighborhood brewpub to the small northwest Indiana city of Whiting. The blue-collar roots of Bulldog run deep with Clark as a steel worker and Kochis as a firefighter. This is the classic story of friends coming together over the love of homebrew and the ambition to have a brewery of one's own.

OWNER
Jeff Kochis, Kevin Clark

HEAD BREWER
Kevin Clark

AVAILABILITY
NW IN

BEST KNOWN FOR
IPAs, classic American styles

DATE FOUNDED
2011

2016 PRODUCTION
800 bbl

20 | 100 | | | • | • | | • | | | 3.3/5

BULLDOG BREWING CO.

PRO TIPS

» A few guest drafts are available here, as is a full bar.

» Try some of the rarely-done styles that Clark puts together, like the Kentucky Common or almost-imperial-strength Bohemian lager.

» The wooden beams adorning the ceiling, and the occasional decorative surfboard, gives the brewpub a homey, unintimidating atmosphere.

» Bulldog's menu offers a bevy of sandwiches, burgers, pizza, pasta, and entrées.

» Thursdays feature a DJ and a raffle. Look for live bands during special brewpub events.

» Five minutes from Horseshoe Casino.

» Hit Whiting's Pierogi Fest in July.

DATE OF VISIT:

MY RATING
☆ ☆ ☆ ☆ ☆

NOTES:

POPULAR BEERS

M	Tu	W	Th	F	S	Su
11a-12a	11a-12a	11a-12a	11a-12a	11a-2a	11a-2a	11a-12a

BYWAY BREWING

FIELD NOTES

Byway Brewing started off in the age old tradition of a bunch of seasoned home brewers and close friends coming together to brew beer. Fast forward to 2013, Dave Toth and Branko Sajn decided to turn that passion into a profession, creating a new destination brewpub in Hammond, IN, an easy jump off the busy I-94 corridor. David and Branko completed the brewpub in 2016 and have created a space where couples, families, and parties alike can enjoy amazing craft beer and food while escaping the buzz of the city.

2825 Carlson Dr.
Hammond, IN 46323
219-844-5468
bywaybrewing.beer

OWNER
Dave Toth, Tom Duszynski, Branko Sajn

HEAD BREWER
Patrick Jones

AVAILABILITY
Chicago, NW IN - limited

BEST KNOWN FOR
IPAs, porters, red ales

DATE FOUNDED
2016

2016 PRODUCTION
522 bbl

RECENT AWARDS
IN Brewers Cup 2016

| 12 | 120 | • | • | • | • | | • | • | | 3.7/5 |

BYWAY BREWING

PRO TIPS

» Dog friendly on the patio only.

» Weekends get busy with private parties so if you can, try to visit during weekdays.

» Chef-driven menu. Try both the octopus and poutine appetizers; you won't be disappointed.

» Atmosphere includes soft rock music and three TVs that don't overwhelm the space (usually tuned to sports).

» Currently, almost all their beers are taproom only (with a few exceptions in town) so make sure to grab a growler or two before leaving.

» Right off the bike path. Make a stop here then continue riding to 3 Floyds.

DATE OF VISIT:

MY RATING
☆ ☆ ☆ ☆ ☆

NOTES:

POPULAR BEERS

M	Tu	W	Th	F	S	Su
11:30-10	11:30-10	11:30-10	11:30-10	11:30-11	11:30-11	11:30-9

THE DEVIL'S TRUMPET BREWING CO.

FIELD NOTES

Make sure to keep your GPS handy when trying to make your way to Merrilville, IN. But once there, you won't regret the journey. Heavy metal over the stereo, beers such as Make It A Cheeseburger IPA and the use of unique ingredients will definitely make this a place you won't forget. Brewmasters and owners Chris Pearson and Bob Lusin decided that after being in the same home brewing club, they wanted to start a brewery. Expect creations and experimentations with recipes that go beyond the traditional style norms.

8250 Utah St.
Merrillville, IN 46410
219-576-7118
**thedevilstrumpet.
com**

OWNER
Steve Carter, Chris
Pearson, Bob Lusin,
Mark Mileusnic

HEAD BREWER
Chris Pearson, Bob
Lusin

AVAILABILITY
IN

BEST KNOWN FOR
IPAs, stouts

DATE FOUNDED
2014

2016 PRODUCTION
400 bbl

KEY EVENTS
Heaven's Court Day
(Jun)

11 | 60 | • | • | | • | | | • | | 4.1/5

THE DEVIL'S TRUMPET BREWING CO.

PRO TIPS

» Dog friendly on the patio only.

» You can grab a beer to go on Sundays even though old Indiana "Blue Laws" still prevent Sunday to go sales most everywhere else.

» If available, try one of their sours or barrel-conditioned beers.

» They offer a beer sampler called Flight of the 11 (all 11 beers on draft), a great option for first timers. But don't worry, that's only about 2.75 pints in volume.

» In the summer they have a beautiful patio and sometimes a food truck if you get hungry! Otherwise, they are bring in your own food.

DATE OF VISIT:

MY RATING
☆ ☆ ☆ ☆ ☆

NOTES:

POPULAR BEERS

M	Tu	W	Th	F	S	Su
3p-9p	3p-9p	3p-9p	3p-9p	3p-11p	12p-11p	12p-8p

NEW OBERPFALZ BREWING

FIELD NOTES

The Oberpfalz region of Bavaria is where the head brewer of New Oberpfalz's family is from, so giving a shout back to the area, bordering the Czech Republic and north of Munich, made sense when starting up this Indiana brewery. Releasing their first brews in 2015, New Oberpfalz specializes in German-style ales and lagers, but works outwards from there to encompass a variety of styles popular to American craft beer fans. New Oberpfalz' flagships are a pale, Helles lager, and a Schwarzbier.

121 E. Main St.
Griffith, IN 46319
219-513-9341
newoberpfalz.com

OWNER
Dan Lehnerer,
Jennifer Lehnerer

HEAD BREWER
Dan Lehnerer

AVAILABILITY
IN

BEST KNOWN FOR
Lagers, IPAs, stouts

DATE FOUNDED
2015

2016 PRODUCTION
429 bbl

KEY EVENTS
Crawfish Boil (May),
Oktoberfest (Sept)

| 12 | 75 | • | • | • | | | • | • | | 4.0/5 |

NEW OBERPFALZ BREWING

PRO TIPS

» Dog friendly on the patio only.

» New Oberpfalz does distribute their beer, but not over the state line. So if you want packaged beer, be prepared to drive to Indiana.

» The brewpub is a quaint, unassuming space on Griffith's main drag that offers around a dozen different house-made beers on draft and in bottle form.

» Picnic tables with sun umbrellas grace the patio when the weather cooperates.

» The menu offers a selection of appetizers, sandwiches, and personal-sized pizzas. The weisswurst is a lovely take on the German-style encased meat served on a pretzel roll.

DATE OF VISIT:

MY RATING
☆ ☆ ☆ ☆ ☆

NOTES:

POPULAR BEERS

M	Tu	W	Th	F	S	Su
closed	3p-10p	3p-10p	3p-10p	11a-10p	11a-10p	11a-7p

POKRO BREWING COMPANY

FIELD NOTES

Classic story here - head brewer and founder Joe Pokropinski (hence the name) has been brewing for over a decade and a half. He began, like many brewers do, with homebrewing. Getting a push from his wife Robyn, who's the business brains of the operation, the pair began this labor of love which culminated in a Valentine's Day 2015 opening. Pokropinski's beers focus on American, English, and Belgian styles, with enough variety on the modest list to keep you from getting bored with the options.

311 N. Broad St.
Griffith, IN 46319
219-924-7950
pokrobrewing.com

OWNER
Joe Pokropinski,
Robyn Pokropinski

HEAD BREWER
Joe Pokropinski

AVAILABILITY
NW IN

BEST KNOWN FOR
Belgian, English

DATE FOUNDED
2015

2016 PRODUCTION
187 bbl

KEY EVENTS
POKtoberfest (Oct)

| 12 | 100 | | | | • | | • | • | | 4.1/5 |

POKRO BREWING COMPANY

PRO TIPS

» The back room of the taproom space advertises "a man-cave feel with jukebox, board games, giant Jenga, boards & bags, vintage multicade, and dartboard."

» Pokro hosts a variety of events at its space, including a painting-and-drinking night, a musical open-mic night, and even a pop-up boutique.

» There is a food menu available, featuring Polish-inspired cuisine, including pierogi, golabki, sausages, and other favorites.

» If you're feeling a little hair of the dog, Pokro offers to turn any brew on the menu into a beer-mosa with a splash (or more if you want it) of orange juice.

DATE OF VISIT:

MY RATING
☆ ☆ ☆ ☆ ☆

NOTES:

POPULAR BEERS

 | Monkey Assasin | Caveman Ale | Cammit!

M	Tu	W	Th	F	S	Su
closed	2p-10p	2p-10p	2p-11p	2p-12a	12p-12a	12p-8p

ST. JOHN MALT BROS. CRAFT BREWERS

FIELD NOTES

St. John Malt Brothers opened in February 2015, with rapid expansion plans and expectations to distribute across the state line into Illinois. The St. John, IN brewery is well on its way to a maximum production of 1,500 barrels per year. Their beers seem to either celebrate clever references to film and other media, or simply celebrate hops. Either way, it's a winning combination for this still very young brewery.

9607 Wicker Ave.
St. John, IN 46373
219-627-4294
sjmaltbros.com

OWNER
Jim Estry, Dan Cox, Dave Witt

HEAD BREWER
Dan Breed

AVAILABILITY
NW IN, Chicago - limited

BEST KNOWN FOR
IPAs, porters, stouts, browns

DATE FOUNDED
2015

2016 PRODUCTION
695 bbl

KEY EVENTS
Ribfest (May), Walleye Palooza (Jul), Prime Rib Smokeout (Jul), Pig Roast (Aug), Crab Boil (Sept)

16 | 47 | • | • | • | • | • | 3.9/5

ST. JOHN MALT BROS. CRAFT BREWERS

PRO TIPS

» Dog friendly on the patio only.

» The inside of the taproom is friendly with some bar seating, but most will be accommodated at the tables of various heights. Some outdoor seating is available on the patriotically-decorated patio.

» The appetizer menu features deep-fried ravioli and what they call a "pint of bacon."

» Bombers and cans of some beers can be had at the pub. All beer, to-go or otherwise, is $2 off on Tuesdays, and growlers are $3 off on Sundays.

» Wine and craft sodas are available.

DATE OF VISIT:

MY RATING
☆ ☆ ☆ ☆ ☆

NOTES:

POPULAR BEERS

M	Tu	W	Th	F	S	Su
3p-11p	3p-11p	3p-11p	3p-11p	2p-12a	11a-12a	11a-9p

WILDROSE BREWING

FIELD NOTES

1104 E. Main St.
Griffith, IN 46319
219-595-5054
**wildrosebrewing.
com**

Wildrose Brewing is built out of a large, re-purposed pole barn space by five friends who bonded over a love of homebrewing in their own garages. Sharing the beers with friends (who must have responded favorably) led to the idea that they should start their own operation, and, well, here we are. Wildrose opened in Griffith, IN in 2015, less than a mile from fellow brewers Pokro and New Oberpfalz. Stouts and hops dominate the draft menu here, with the occasional pilsner and wheat ale peeking through.

OWNER
Kevin Krippel,
Tony Nicola, Karen
DeJong, David
DeJong

HEAD BREWER
David DeJong

AVAILABILITY
NW IN

BEST KNOWN FOR
IPAs, pales, stouts,
wheat ales

DATE FOUNDED
2014

2016 PRODUCTION
350 bbl

12 | 100 | • | • | | • | | • | • | | 3.9/5

WILDROSE BREWING

PRO TIPS

» Dog friendly on the patio only.

» Roses, thorns, and skulls adorn the front of the Wildrose facility like it was a long lost hard rock album cover from the 1980s.

» There's a shaded patio perfect for the sunniest of summer days when you've forgotten your sunblock.

» The food menu is small but adequate, featuring sandwiches, burgers, and appetizers all meant to soak up a bit of the booze and raise your blood pressure ever so slightly.

» Live music on Fridays.

» Don't overlook the guest cider on draft.

DATE OF VISIT:

MY RATING
☆ ☆ ☆ ☆ ☆

NOTES:

POPULAR BEERS

| Big Sexy | Mad Cow | Mornin' James | Hop Side Of The Moon |

| M | Tu | W | Th | F | S | Su |
| 3p-11p | 3p-11p | 3p-11p | 3p-11p | 3p-12a | 12p-12a | 12p-8p |

WINDMILL BREWING

FIELD NOTES

2121 Gettler St.
Dyer, IN 46311
219-440-2189
windmillbrew.com

Windmills are often seen as a national symbol of The Netherlands, where they were used for everything from scooping and draining the wetlands to grinding grain to flour in mills. In Dyer, IN, the Windmill is also the symbol of Scott Vander Griend and Justin Verburg, two friends of Dutch extraction, who, after years of years of friendship and homebrewing, decided to start Windmill Brewing in 2015. Their goal is to offer craft beer fans brews that aren't necessarily assaults on the palate, but a wide range of balanced flavors that continually push tradition instead.

OWNER
Scott Vander Griend,
Justin Verburg

HEAD BREWER
Justin, Verburg

AVAILABILITY
NW IN

BEST KNOWN FOR
Belgians, IPAs, pales, stouts

DATE FOUNDED
2015

2016 PRODUCTION
260 bbl

KEY EVENTS
Anniversary Party
(Aug)

| 14 | 55 | | • | | ∞ | | | | • | | 4.2/5 |

WINDMILL BREWING

PRO TIPS

» There's a three beer per person per day limit at Windmill, so keep that in mind when examining their list of 8-10 beers.

» Cans to-go are usually available on site, but check ahead for up to date availability.

» The space itself is small-ish, but charming, with a couple bar seats, a chalkboard draft list, stamped metal tables, and a characterful mix of chairs.

» A giant Jenga game set is featured prominently in the taproom.

» Keep your eye out for the brewery's two cats; you might see them about.

DATE OF VISIT:

MY RATING
☆ ☆ ☆ ☆ ☆

NOTES:

POPULAR BEERS

Single Double Tripel	Galac-tose	Pale Dutch Boy	40 Hulking Giants

M	Tu	W	Th	F	S	Su
3p-10p	3p-10p	3p-10p	3p-10p	3p-11p	11a-11p	closed

AREA EVENTS CALENDAR

Throughout the year, the greater Chicago area hosts a variety of industry events that the truly "beermiscuous" should not miss. Below is our list of highlights.

JANUARY
- » Chicago Ale Fest Winter Edition (Navy Pier)

FEBRUARY
- » Naperville Ale Fest Winter Edition (Frontier Park)

MARCH
- » Windy City Brewhaha (Revel Fulton Market)
- » Chicago Beer Festival (Field Museum)

APRIL/MAY
- » Dark Lord Day (3 Floyds, Munster, IN)

MAY
- » Chicago Beer Classic (Soldier Field)
- » Craft & Cuisine (Park at Wrigley)
- » Beer Under Glass (Garfield Park Conservatory)
- » Chicago Craft Beer Week (various locations)
- » South Side Craft Beer Fest (Baderbräu)

JUNE
- » Chicago Ale Fest (Grant Park)
- » Two Brothers Summer Festival (Aurora)
- » Ravenswood On Tap (Ravenswood)
- » Craft Brews at the Zoo (Lincoln Park Zoo)
- » Beermiscuous Anniversary (Lakeview)

- » Morton Arboretum Craft Beer Festival (Lisle)

JULY
- » Barrington Brew Fest (Barrington)
- » Square Roots Festival (Lincoln Square)
- » Chicago Craft Beer Fest (Lincoln Park)
- » New Belgium Tour de Fat (Northerly Island)
- » Naperville Ale Fest (Naper Settlement)

AUGUST
- » Welles Park Craft Beer Fest (Welles Park)
- » Beer & BBQ Challenge (Old Irving Park)
- » Great Taste of the Midwest (Madison, WI)
- » Oak Park Micro Brew Review (Oak Park)

SEPTEMBER
- » 312 Urban Block Party (Fulton Market)
- » Lagunitas Beer Circus (Douglas Park)

OCTOBER
- » Festiv-Ale (Fulton Market)
- » Munster Ale Fest (Munster, IN)

NOVEMBER
- » BeerHoptacular (Cinespace Film Studios)
- » Festival of Wood & Barrel Aged Beers—FoBAB (UIC Forum)

JUST-MISSED BREWERIES

The following breweries are expected to open their taprooms/brewpubs very soon, but unfortunately just missed our print date for inclusion in this year's guide.

CITY NORTH

METROPOLITAN BREWING
3057 North Rockwell, Chicago, IL 60618; metrobrewing.com

CITY NEAR LOOP

GREAT CENTRAL BREWING
221 N. Wood St., Chicago, IL 60612; greatcentralbrewing.com

LO REZ BREWING
2101 S. Carpenter St., Chicago, IL 60608; lorezbrewing.com

MARZ COMMUNITY BREWING
3630 S. Iron St., Chicago, IL 60609; marzbrewing.com

OFF COLOR BREWING
1460 N. Kingsbury, Chicago, IL 60642; offcolorbrewing.com

CITY SOUTH

OPEN OUTCRY BREWING
10934 S. Western, Chicago, IL 60643; openoutcrybrewing.com

SUBURBS NORTH

MACUSHLA BREWING
1516 East Lake Ave, Glenview, IL 60025; facebook.com/macushlabeer/

SUBURBS NORTHWEST

FLESK BREWING
200 Applebee St., Barrington, IL 60010; fleskbrewing.com

SUBURBS WEST

MORE BREWING CO.
126 S. Villa Ave, Villa Park, IL 60181; facebook.com/morebrewingco/

SHORT FUSE BREWING
5000 N. River Rd., Schiller Park, IL 60176; shortfusebrewing.com

SUBURBS SOUTH

SOUNDGROWLER BREWING
8201 183rd St., Tinley Park, IL 60487; soundgrowler.com

SUBURBS NW INDIANA

OFF SQUARE BREWING
11000 Deleware Pkwy, Crown Point, IN 46307; offsquarebrewing.com

	ABV	Seats	🪑	🪑	🌳	🐕	👶	◯	🥨	MENU	Ⓟ	🚲	⭐	Rating
CITY NORTH														
Andersonville	16	76	•			•	•			•				3.3/5
Band of Bohemia	8	150				•				•	•		•	3.8/5
Begyle	13	60			•	•				•	•		•	4.0/5
Burnt City	25	200	•			•	•			•			•	3.6/5
Corridor	6	90	•	•		•	•						•	3.8/5
Dovetail	18	90	•	•		•	•		•		•	•	•	4.1/5
Dryhop	6	75	•			•	•			•			•	3.8/5
Empirical	12	95		•		•	•						•	3.9/5
Greenstar	12	150	•	•		•				•			•	3.5/5
Half Acre	14	70				•							•	4.1/5
CITY NORTHWEST														
Alarmist	12	70				•			•		•		•	3.8/5
Hopewell	10	99			•	•				•			•	3.8/5
Old Irving	20	225				•	•			•	•		•	3.9/5
Piece	16	275				•	•						•	3.9/5
Revolution	16	281				•	•						•	4.5/5
CITY NEAR LOOP														
All Rise	20	300	•	•		•				•	•		•	3.8/5
Alulu	30	75	•			•							•	NA/5
Baderbräu	10	162				•	•			•			•	3.9/5
Birreria	9	50				•	•			•			•	3.7/5
Cruz Blanca	12	67				•	•			•			•	3.8/5
Forbidden Root	16	258	•			•	•			•			•	4.0/5
Gino's	11	340	•			•	•			•			•	3.6/5
Goose Island	16	100				•	•			•			•	3.9/5
Haymarket	24	400	•			•	•			•	•		•	3.7/5
Lagunitas	16	250				•	•			•	•	•	•	4.1/5
Mad Mouse	24	205	•			•	•			•			•	3.7/5
Moody Tongue	12	95				•	•		•			•	•	4.0/5
Motor Row	8	200		•		•	•		•			•	•	4.0/5
On Tour	12	98				•	•						•	4.4/5
Vice District	16	99			•	•	•						•	3.8/5
CITY SOUTH														
Horse Thief Hollow	12	160				•	•			•	•		•	3.8/5
Whiner	10	100			•	•	•						•	4.1/5
SUBURBS NORTH														
Half Day	40	400	•			•	•			•	•		•	3.5/5
Kings & Convicts	8	30	•	•		•	•			•			•	NA/5
Lake Bluff	14	60				•	•			•			•	3.8/5
Mickey Finn's	16	300	•			•	•		•	•			•	3.6/5
Only Child	8	50	•	•		•	•	•		•			•	4.1/5
Peckish Pig	12	180	•			•	•		•				•	3.7/5
Prairie Krafts	12	55	•	•		•	•	•			•		•	3.9/5
Sketchbook	12	45				•	•						•	4.0/5
Smylie Bros.	16	290	•			•	•	•		•			•	3.6/5
Temperance	12	300	•			•	•			•			•	4.0/5
Ten Ninety	20	91	•	•		•	•			•	•		•	3.7/5
Une Année	12	45	•	•		•	•			•			•	4.3/5
Zümbier	13	30	•			•	•			•			•	4.2/5
SUBURBS NORTHWEST														
Bosacki's	12	69				•	•			•	•		•	4.1/5
Crystal Lake	12	180	•			•	•			•			•	3.8/5
Emmett's	12	170	•	•		•	•	•		•	•		•	3.6/5
Light the Lamp	10	50				•	•				•		•	3.8/5

									(P)		
The Lucky Monk	12	400	•		•	•			•		3.7/5
Mikerphone	8	45			•	•				•	4.4/5
Scorched Earth	12	50	•	•	•	•			•		4.0/5
Side Lot	16	60	•	•	•	•		•	•		3.7/5
Tighthead	16	140	•		•	•			•		4.0/5
Village Vintner	12	125	•		•	•			•		3.5/5
Wild Onion	18	135	•		•	•			•		3.6/5
SUBURBS WEST											
5 Rabbit	8	80	•	•	•	•			•		3.8/5
Alter	12	106	•	•	•	•	•		•		4.0/5
Blue Nose	10	250	•	•	•	•			•		4.0/5
Buckledown	10	75	•		•	•			•		3.8/5
Church Street	8	150	•		•	•			•		3.9/5
Exit Strategy	16	140	•		•	•		•	•		3.9/5
Flapjack	8	60			•	•			•		NA/5
Imperial Oak	20	175	•		•	•			•		4.2/5
Itasca	14	100	•		•	•			•		4.0/5
Kinslahger	12	48			•	•	•		•		4.3/5
Lunar	17	105			•	•			•		3.9/5
Miskatonic	10	115	•	•	•	•			•		3.9/5
Myths & Legends	10	40			•	•			•		4.0/5
Noon Whistle	10	80	•		•	•			•		3.9/5
Oak Park	16	100	•		•	•			•		3.3/5
Skeleton Key	8	100			•	•			•		4.0/5
SUBURBS FAR WEST											
BBGB	20	210	•		•	•		•	•		3.6/5
Dry City	6	25	•		•	•			•		4.0/5
Hopvine	32	277	•	•	•	•			•		3.5/5
Metal Monkey	16	90		•	•	•			•		4.0/5
Nevin's	20	300	•		•	•			•		3.2/5
Penrose	15	105	•		•	•			•	•	3.9/5
Solemn Oath	10	80			•	•			•		3.9/5
Two Brothers	18	250	•		•	•			•		3.8/5
Werk Force	13	50		•	•	•			•		4.3/5
SUBURBS SOUTH											
350	20	120			•	•			•		3.9/5
Arrowhead	12	200	•		•	•			•		3.8/5
Blue Island	12	56	•	•	•	•			•		4.0/5
Evil Horse	14	150	•	•	•	•			•		3.8/5
Flossmoor Station	16	240	•		•	•			•		3.8/5
Hailstorm	16	200		•	•	•			•		4.1/5
One Trick Pony	24	50	•	•	•	•			•		3.9/5
Pollyanna	12	46	•	•	•	•			•		3.9/5
Tribes	42	150	•		•	•			•		3.9/5
SUBURBS NORTHWEST INDIANA											
18th Street	9	60			•	•			•	•	4.0/5
3 Floyds	20	75			•	•			•		3.9/5
Bulldog	20	100			•	•			•		3.3/5
Byway	12	120	•	•	•	•			•		3.7/5
Devil's Trumpet	11	60	•	•	•	•			•		4.1/5
New Oberpfalz	12	75	•	•	•	•			•		4.0/5
Pokro	12	100			•	•			•		4.1/5
St. John Malt Bros.	16	47	•	•	•	•			•		3.9/5
Wildrose	12	100	•	•	•	•			•		3.9/5
Windmill	14	55	•	•	•	•			•		4.2/5

CONGRATS!

You've completed your journey of Chicago's taprooms and brewpubs, or maybe you're just tired of all the travel and need a respite. Either way, join us for a drink and tell us about your favorites.

2812 N. Lincoln Ave.
Chicago, IL 60657
beermiscuous.com

Beermiscuous carries over 350 different craft beer brands (16 on draft and the rest bottles and cans), with a vast majority of these locally focused. So think of us as your taproom of taprooms under one roof. And don't forget about all the great Chicago breweries that don't have taprooms—we carry those too (like Spiteful, Pipeworks, and Hop Butcher for the World just to name a few). See you soon!

M	Tu	W	Th	F	S	Su
1p-11p	1p-11p	1p-11p	1p-11p	1p-12a	12p-12a	12p-8p

Photo Credit: Timothy Musho

Photo Credit: Timothy M